God Is in the Laundry Room

A WOMEN'S BIBLE STUDY

BY SUSAN SENECHAL

CONCORDIA PUBLISHING HOUSE • SAINT LOUIS

To Mark: Your love and encouragement are priceless treasures.
Thanks for helping me to hit "send."

And for the women who share my Tuesday mornings:
As we encourage and love one another, share insights and grow together,
I can't imagine Tuesday mornings without you.

Therefore, encourage one another and build one another up,
just as you are doing. 1 Thessalonians 5:11

TABLe oF CoNteNTS

BEFORE YOU BEGIN THIS STUDY

I was a reluctant Bible study attendee. *I don't have time,* I thought. *I have too much to do.* It wasn't until the fifth or sixth invitation that I finally agreed to attend.

I was an even more reluctant Bible study leader. But when the leader of our group moved out of state, a few of the women suggested that since I am a former teacher, I take over as leader. I hesitated. (That's not quite true; at first I said a flat-out no.) Like Moses, I said, "What if they don't believe me or won't listen to me?" Like Moses, I made excuses about my inability to speak in front of a group. As a former English teacher, that wouldn't seem to be the case, but standing up in front of high school students is one thing; these women were my peers. And *women* are another story.

Like Moses, I said, "Please, God, send somebody else."

And then, like Moses, I heard God speak to my heart: "I will help you to speak and teach you what to say." Now, more than ten years later, I cannot imagine beginning a Tuesday morning without my Bible study group and the laughter, friendship, and a look at God's Word it brings.

As a wife and a mother, I long to see lasting significance in the repetitive chores I do. I long to know there is more to life than an endless grocery list and reappearing fuzz balls under the bed. Because I work part time outside the home, my free time is in short commodity and is, therefore, precious to me. I want to spend my time with things of significance, and I found that significance in the words of Jeremiah 29:13: "You will seek Me and find Me, when you seek Me with all your heart." When I sought Him in my daily tasks, I found God everywhere, even in the laundry room.

This Bible study began, literally, with a purple crayon, just as I describe in the first session. Within forty-eight hours of my laundry nightmare, God had clearly spoken to my heart about confession and about how He has thoroughly redeemed my sin-stained life and made me whiter than snow. The other lessons, too, began with daily tasks and mishaps, as God heard the cry of my heart for purpose and significance. It is my prayer now that as you begin this study, God will lead you to see Him in your daily routines as well.

Designed as a women's small-group study, each lesson in this book goes beyond merely "looking up the right answer." Instead, this study urges you to make personal application of the passages to your life—not as an afterthought at the end of the lesson, but as integral throughout the study.

Each lesson opens with a "before you begin" question. Don't miss the opportunity to share a little bit of yourself with the others in your group. As you open up to one another about the trivial, you'll form friendships and relationships that provide opportunity to share the significant.

This study is more than filling in the blanks with the right words from a Bible passage. Although the lessons don't require a vast storehouse of biblical knowledge, each lesson does use cross-referencing, and, springing from my own love of language, lessons explore the original Greek and Hebrew words to help you gain a deeper understanding of the passages involved. Don't let that scare you; in fact, you may become a language lover too.

My desire is that these studies will challenge you, whether you are a new Christian or a lifelong believer, to apply God's Word to your own situation. I hope your small group is a place where you feel free to share your opinions and questions and a place where you are able to learn from the other women. I believe God is ready and waiting to meet you . . . in the laundry room and in every place you spend your day.

> . . . For "In Him we live and move and have our being."
> Acts 17:28a

SUGGESTIONS FOR SMALL-GROUP PARTICIPANTS

1. Begin small-group time with prayer.
2. Everyone should feel free to express her thoughts. Comments shared in the small group should remain confidential unless you have received permission to share them outside your group.
3. If your meeting time does not allow you to discuss all of the questions for the week, the leader should choose the questions most meaningful to the group.
4. Close by sharing concerns and prayer requests, then praying together.

THE COLOR PURPLE

A LAUNDRY LESSON
FROM GOD—PART 1

Before you begin:
What is your best laundry story
or your worst laundry nightmare?

It was a laundry nightmare. First one T-shirt, then another, covered with purple spots. Next came skirts, shorts, socks, underwear—all covered by "purple pox" as they came out of the dryer. Nearly everything my daughter owned, or at least would wear, was in that load of laundry. And now, because of a rogue purple crayon, it all appeared to be ruined. I had images of my six-year-old running around naked all summer.

I fired out an urgent e-mail—"HELP!!!"—to just about everyone on my address list, everyone who was or ever had been a parent. *Surely someone will have a solution,* I thought. *I can't afford to get her a whole new wardrobe!* The replies came quickly. Some felt my pain; others pointed me to some stain-fighting tips on Web sites. Still others told me stories from their own spotted pasts. I began to make a plan of attack.

My first strategy was WD-40, recommended by the Crayola Web site. *Who better to know crayon spots?* I asked myself. This treatment proved to be time prohibitive; with hundreds of spots to treat, I figured I'd be at this job all summer. Plus, the fumes were making me a bit dizzy (or was that ditzy?). It was time to move on to plan B.

I reevaluated some of the advice I had been given, combined a couple of methods, and came up with a chemical cocktail I hoped would work. At least it couldn't make it any worse, I reasoned. It amused me somewhat that for years, as I talked with friends about household chores we despised, laundry usually showed up on their lists, but never on mine. I didn't mind running the clothes through, folding them, or putting them away, then finding another pile before the job was complete. "Just don't expect me to get out any spots," I'd say. Now I was facing the spottiest challenge of my housekeeping career.

To my surprise, the first load came out of the washer spot free. (This was the WD-40 load that I'd believed would take all summer to treat.) The second load with purple freckles got my chemical cocktail.* Most of these clothes, too, came out clean, although a few items needed to be retreated.

Thrilled with the results, I tried the third load—the clothes I considered too far gone because of the size or number of stains. But they, too, came out spotless. *How can it be,* I thought, *as badly stained as they were, that they could come out clean?*

When I take a step back and think about the bigger picture of my life, I realize that I'm often guilty of treating my Christianity the way I treat the laundry: I don't mind it; in fact, I sometimes enjoy it because I can do it while I'm doing something else. It runs in the background. It's a routine task.

Just don't ask me to get any spots out. I like to worship, participate in Bible study, and think about and discuss things spiritual. I'm all for listening to Christian music, reading Christian books, and hanging out with Christian friends. But I'd really prefer to overlook the spots of sin in my life. I'd like to forget that the stain from my "purple crayon of selfishness" runs through the load of my life or that the "green marker of greed" touches and stains everything as it tumbles around in my heart.

Seeing stains on my clothes reminds me that my life isn't perfect. But having to deal with that load of purple-spotted laundry taught me that I cannot ignore the stain of sin. I can either cry over spilled milk (or melted crayon), or I can get busy and do something about it.

BiBLe STUDY QUeSTi°NS

1. Read 1 John 1:8–9. What does the apostle John remind us is the first step in doing spiritual laundry?

2. a. "If we say we are without sin." Romans 3:10–18 lays out some of the sins we are especially good at. What are they?

What a list! "No one seeks for God. All have turned aside . . ." (vv. 11–12). " 'Their throat is an open grave; they use their tongues to deceive. . . . Their mouth is full of curses and bitterness' " (vv. 13–14). And that's not even the complete list in Romans, let alone the complete list in our present life! Much of this list boils down to how we use our tongues—the words that come out of our mouths.

When we evaluate the sin in our life, it's so easy to think that we're relatively clean. We don't murder, commit adultery, or steal. Yet Jesus says, "What comes out of the mouth proceeds from the heart, and this defiles a person" (Matthew 15:18). If we carefully examine the words we speak, we see that they don't always reflect a pure heart.

b. What does the Lord say through the prophet Isaiah concerning our words and our hearts? See Isaiah 29:13.

Paul's exhortation to the Romans didn't begin with our word sins, either. "No one **seeks** for God. . . ." (Romans 3:11). The Greek word here is *ekzeteo*. It means "to seek after diligently," but also "to crave, demand, inquire, and even worship." Do

I carefully and prayerfully seek God? Do I crave Him? Is my heart set on worshiping Him? Or am I giving God lip service without giving Him my heart?

c. The words of David in Psalm 19:14 can be a quick, memorable prayer for this area of your life. Write them here in your own words:

3. a. "We **deceive** ourselves" (1 John 1:8). The Greek word used here is *planao,* which means "to cause to roam" (from safety, truth, virtue). Its Greek root means "delusion, error." In what ways have you deluded yourself about a sin in your life? How has this caused you to roam from the safety, truth, and peace of a God-pleasing life?

b. The first time the word *deceive* is used in the ESV Bible is in Genesis 3:13. Eve says, "The serpent deceived me." The Hebrew word used there is *nasha*—"to lead astray." This word is identical to the Hebrew word for "usury"—loan sharking. The implication? You may get what you want for now, but the price to be paid later is extremely high. How have you been deceived into a sinful behavior?

c. "If we **confess** our sin" (1 John 1:9). The Greek word here is *homologeo.* This word is formed from two Greek words, *homo,* which means "same," and *logos,* which means "word." It does not mean to merely repeat the same words over and over, as we may do if we just thoughtlessly utter a prescribed confession. *Homologeo* is not a simple, mindless repetition of what someone else has said; it is agreeing with the statement and taking it to heart. In fact, it is agreeing with God, saying, in effect, "Lord God, You see this as a sin, and I say the same."

Rarely is *homologeo* used in the New Testament to talk about confession of sins. Rather, it is often translated "profess" or "acknowledge," frequently in the context of boldly declaring Christ (Matthew 10:32; Acts 24:14). How does this relate to confessing sin? Just as we are to "tell [it] plainly" (the Matthew 7:23 NIV use of the same Greek word) that Jesus is Lord, so, too, are we to declare, confess, and acknowledge plainly that we have sinned.

Think about an unconfessed sin you may have. How does it stain your life? If you're comfortable doing so, write that confession here. Otherwise, take it to God in prayer.

It is sometimes easy for me to make a blanket confession in church each Sunday, to acknowledge generically that I am a sinner in need of salvation. But there is great benefit in confessing the sin plainly, admitting that it was because I was full of pride, for example, that I was angry with my children today because I thought they made me look bad to my neighbors. Then I can move past the guilt ("I am a terrible parent") and begin to deal with the cause ("I need to work on my pride issues").

4. a. David clearly spells out the benefit of confession. According to Psalm 32:3–5, what is it?

b. How does Proverbs 28:13 echo this thought?

Before receiving Holy Communion, we are to examine ourselves (1 Corinthians 11:28). Acts 3:19 tells us to "Repent . . . and turn to God, so that your sins may be wiped out, that times of **refreshing** may come from the Lord" (NIV, emphasis added). The Greek word is *abnapsuxis*, which means "a recovery of breath, revival." It's as if as long as we have unconfessed sin, we are holding our breath. Maybe we are waiting for the proverbial other shoe to drop. Only after we have confessed and received forgiveness can we breathe freely again.

After our confession, we are offered absolution—a declaration or assurance of forgiveness releasing us from the guilt of those sins. 1 John 1:8–9 tells us this: "If we confess our sins, [God] is faithful and just to forgive us our sins and to cleanse us from all unrighteousness." When the pastor absolves us of our sins during the Divine Service, it is as if we have just dealt with Jesus Christ Himself. The forgiveness is free and final.

He will "cleanse us from all unrighteousness" (v. 9). Read Mark 1:40–42 below. The Greek word for **cleanse** is used three times in this short passage.

> *And a leper came to Him, imploring Him, and kneeling said to Him, "If You will, You can **make** me **clean**." Moved with pity, He stretched out His hand and touched him and said to him, "I will; be **clean**." And immediately the leprosy left him and he was **made clean**.*

Notice that God's healing action is instantaneous. At Jesus' command, the man was healed. No waiting. The same is true for us when we confess our sins. We hear the Words of Absolution in the Divine Service: God forgives us our sins and cleanses us from all unrighteousness, from anything that we have done in thought, word or deed—if we confess those sins.

The first step, then, in doing our spiritual laundry is acknowledging that the spots exist and that we put them there. In Psalm 139:23–24, David shows us how to go one step further when he asks God to point out the hidden spots, the ones he doesn't see easily or the ones that don't really seem like a sin—worry, anxiety, doubt—but which nonetheless show a lack of faith or trust in God.

5. Peter heard Jesus make this connection in Matthew 14:30–31. All of the disciples heard it as well in Mark 4:37–40. In each of these cases, what is Jesus' response to their worry?

It would be good to pray with David the words from Psalm 139:23–24: "Search me, O God, and know my heart! Try me and know my thoughts! And see if there be any grievous way in me, and lead me in the way everlasting!"

"See if there be any **grievous** way in me" (v. 24). Here, the NIV Bible says "offensive," and the KJV translates this as "wicked." But even more fascinating is its Hebrew root. The primary root of the Hebrew word for "wicked" (*otseb*) is from *atsab*, "to carve," that is, "to fabricate or fashion." From it also comes the Hebrew word *etseb*, which can be translated as "idol."

When we begin to see anxiety and worry as something that causes grief to God, something that is offensive and wicked, an idol even, it becomes so much more apparent that it is not a spot we can live with or remove by our own effort.

6. According to the following passages, what should we do with idols (and therefore the idol of worry)?

a. Deuteronomy 7:5

b. 1 Samuel 12:21 (The word here for "idol" is translated "empty things" in the ESV.)

7. Even people who worship the triune God can find themselves worshiping idols. See 2 Kings 17:41. What is the implication for our children or grandchildren?

8. Jeremiah's favorite word to describe idols is "worthless." (This is especially apparent in the NIV.) In Jeremiah 2:11, notice what he says we have done, which can easily apply to worry.

This passage is quite clear in the NIV: "My people have exchanged their Glory for worthless idols." This thought ties in to Psalm 106:20–21. When we exchange glory for worry, what have we forgotten?

9. a. And we all know the story of Jonah. He was worried about what would happen if he went to Nineveh, so he instead chose to flee in the opposite direction. Read his prayer from the belly of the fish (Jonah 2:1–9), concentrating on verse 8 as it applies to the idol of worry. What does Jonah say?

Again, I like this passage as translated in the NIV: "Those who cling to worthless idols forfeit the grace that could be theirs." When I see worry as an idol, I can recognize its powerlessness. Isaiah, too, declares the worthlessness of idols, carved of wood, of the same materials that we throw into the fire (Isaiah 44:14–19).

b. What does Jesus remind us about the worthlessness of worry in Matthew 6:27?

10. So we now know worry is a sin. It's offensive to God, and it's even called "wicked" and "idolatrous." It's a spot we cannot live with. And like a stain caused by coffee or tea—or crayons—it persists even after we've treated it. Is there a spot remover that works? What does God tell us in the following passages?

a. Psalm 55:22

b. 1 Peter 5:7

c. Philippians 4:6–7

Perhaps a more effective treatment is to replace our anxious thoughts with other thoughts. Find a passage (may I suggest 1 Chronicles 16:25–31?) to read and meditate on when you are tempted to dwell on something that makes you anxious. You might copy the verse onto an index card and keep it in your purse so you can pull it out when you need to. Or, maybe even better, you could memorize the verse so you'll have it as a constant comfort.

11. Like Scotchgard for your soul, focusing on God's attributes can keep the spot from setting in the first place. God's Word can be a stain barrier. In the end, we can be certain and confident that we are spot free.

According to 1 Corinthians 6:11, what has happened to the spotted you, the you that is covered with sin, spotted and "beyond redemption," as was my third load of spotted clothes?

Although I am unable to make myself clean—to remove my own spots—through Jesus Christ, in the waters of Baptism, God has taken even that which appears beyond redemption and made it thoroughly clean. In the cleansing waters of Baptism, the old Adam (or perhaps the "old Eve") in me dies, the part of me that is sinful from birth. The new person is born—not out of the womb, but out of the waters of Baptism. I am born again, as Jesus says, "of water and the Spirit" (John 3:5). This is all so that we may "walk in newness of life" (Romans 6:4). Because of Jesus' love for me, because He gave Himself up for me, because He washed me in the waters of Baptism, I am without spot or wrinkle, holy and blameless before God (Ephesians 5:25–27). That's cleansed, restored, made new—and wrinkle free! That's you and me, in Jesus Christ!

*Spray Zout on each spot, then wash in 1 c. Tide laundry detergent and 1 c. baking soda in hot water. Then wash a second time after a 30-minute presoak in Oxiclean®. My clothes may have come out faded and too small, but I was determined to get them clean!

THE COLOR PURPLE

A LAUNDRY LESSON
FROM GOD—PART 2

I have a friend whose children began doing their own laundry when they were in elementary school, by age 10. It's a rite of passage. My own daughter, now age 9, sometimes likes to help me with the laundry. She likes to pour the detergent, bleach, and softener into the dispenser, although I find myself checking her amounts, fearing that an *I Love Lucy* episode could play itself out in my laundry room and we will have soap bubbles everywhere. She's a firm believer in "more is more" and "if a little is good, a lot is better."

Not the case for me. I remember that when I was a teenager, my mother took me into the basement where our washing machine was and showed me how it worked. But other than folding a basket of clothes every now and then, I cannot remember doing my own laundry until I went to college. And then, since I was a penny pincher, there was no sorting of colors or fabrics into separate loads. I stuffed as much as would fit in the Laundromat® washing machine, added detergent, and dropped in the quarters. Once a month. Whether I needed to or not. (Just kidding about that last part.)

When I was younger, I was never particularly concerned with how my clothes looked. My mom took care of those details. But as a frugal mom with responsibility for my family's well-being, that load of purple-spotted laundry meant it would be much more economical to get the clothes clean than to buy my daughter a new wardrobe. So I took care of those details.

Even after the spots were removed, Crayola's Web site reminded me, it was necessary to clean my dryer barrel as well, or my next load would also be affected. This was especially important since the laundry had actually become stained in the dryer when the crayon melted. (No, I didn't miss all those spots when I transferred the load to the dryer—they weren't there yet. But I could have—I rarely remember to look at a spot I have treated to see if it has come out in the wash before throwing the clothes into the dryer.) It wasn't a difficult task, but it did take some time to get to the source of the problem and clean it thoroughly.

That advice is good, not just for my laundry, but for my life as well. I am reminded that I not only need to treat the stains of sin, but I need just the right application of just the right treatment to remove what caused the stains in the first place. I need to deal not just with the results of the problem (although sometimes that's a big task in and of itself), but also to get to the root cause, or the problem will just reappear. And I know that sin that is hidden in my life will soon manifest itself in other areas. Habits and behaviors that I keep hidden from my husband, for example, can quickly cause a breakdown in communication, which might lead to resentment, displeasure, depression, and the like.

A stain is a problem until it's treated—and the sooner the better! When a problem lingers, it often "sets in," like an old stain. It's easier to deal with a problem when it's fresh; it's easier to correct a behavior or attitude *before* it becomes habitual and causes further division or hurt. If that sin remains hidden, it becomes like that crayon residue in the dryer—affecting every load of laundry that comes after. In the same way, when we have an unconfessed sin, everything else in our lives is affected.

This is why confession comes at the beginning of our worship service. At the start of the Divine Service, we call upon the name of the Lord (remembering our Baptism—our washing), and we confess to Him that we are stained by sin and need His mercy and grace. "If we confess our sins, He is faithful and just to forgive us our sins and to cleanse us from all unrighteousness" (1 John 1:9). Then, through the pastor, by the Gospel, we are absolved of all our sin—stain free!

BiBLe STUDY QUeSTiONS

1. In last week's lesson, we talked about the benefits of confession. David goes into detail about life without confession in Psalm 32. Read verses 3–4. What happens when we don't confess or acknowledge our sins?

Charash, **"keeping silent,"** is an interesting word in the Hebrew text. Among other meanings, we find "to fabricate, devise [in a bad way], to let alone, to conceal, to be deaf, all with the idea of secrecy." In 2 Samuel 13, you can read the story of Amnon, Tamar, and Absalom, all children of David. When Amnon raped Tamar, Absalom found out and told Tamar to *charash*, to be quiet, to keep silence, to hold her peace. Meanwhile, Absalom's hatred for his brother festered (v. 22), and for two years he devised a plan of revenge, which ultimately resulted in Amnon's death.

Charash, then, implies more than just not confessing the sin, but actively working to cover it up by fabricating lies and keeping secrets. Sometimes the one you are lying to is yourself, as you try to keep the sin hidden from others and a secret from God.

In the same way, the **"bones"** David refers to in Psalm 32:3 are translated from the Hebrew *etsem*, and are more than his skeletal structure. The Hebrew word here means "body, substance, strength, life."

2. What imagery does David use in verse 4 to describe his life while keeping sin silent?

While Psalm 32 is talking about wasting away in guilt, the psalmist uses very similar words when being attacked and surrounded by very real physical enemies in 22:15: "My strength is dried up like a potsherd, and my tongue sticks to my jaws; You lay me in the dust of death." Notice that the body's reaction to both a physical enemy and an emotional one (guilt) is the same: the body wasting away, strength being sapped, feeling God's heavy hand. The suffering, then, from unconfessed sin is real and profound. Just as leaving the dryer barrel untouched would only cause the crayon stain to affect other loads of laundry, doing nothing is not an option in your spiritual life. Ignoring sin is a deliberate action, a choice on our part that separates us from God and places us in a dry and weary land.

Are your bones dried up and wasting away because of hidden, unconfessed sin? Don't let the enemy deceive you into believing that because what you've left unconfessed is not of "biblical proportions," it is not important. He wants you to ignore the sin so it can continue to destroy you and separate you from God. Unconfessed sin can lead to guilt and shame and wasting away. Are you hiding what you are eating or drinking or buying from your spouse or friends, embarrassed and ashamed of what they'll think of you? Do you make excuses for where the day went when you know you were sucked in for hours to the World Wide Web? Satan could be building a wall of guilt and shame between you and your family, and your bones are getting drier and drier.

3. Do we give up hope? No! God brought the prophet Ezekiel to a land filled with dried bones. Read Ezekiel 37:1–10.

a. In verse 3, what is God's question to Ezekiel and Ezekiel's answer?

b. What does God have Ezekiel do next? (See vv. 4–6.)

c. Read verse 10; what is the final result?

Although this prophecy depicts the children of Israel as dried up and dead because they are cut off from God, the application is not lost on our own dried bones. Only through the Word of God and the Spirit of God can life return to our bones that have dried up in the silence, guilt, and shame of hidden sin, cut off from God by our own choices.

Just as we thirst for water when we have an absence of water, so, too, we thirst for God when we feel His absence. The prophet Amos puts it this way: "'Behold, the days are coming,' declares the Lord GOD, 'when I will send a famine on the land— not a famine of bread, nor a thirst for water, but of hearing the words of the LORD'" (Amos 8:11). We feel a thirst for God when we feel His absence, or when we miss His presence. That feeling comes from a separation from God, and the separation comes from unconfessed sin.

When we confess our sins to God, we are acknowledging our separation from God and our thirst for Him. In Psalm 63:1, David acknowledges that he is living in a wilderness without God: "O God, You are my God; earnestly I seek You; my soul thirsts for You; my flesh faints for You, as in a dry and weary land where there is no water."

Jesus, in turn, tells us, "If anyone thirsts, let him come to Me and drink" (John 7:37). If we want life-giving water from a well that will never be dry, we need only come to Him.

4. Don't miss the blessing of acknowledging your sins and confessing them. Read Psalm 32:5 and rest in it for a minute before we move on. Although this is meant to be a personal time, share anything that you might wish.

David prayed a "spiritual laundry" prayer in Psalm 51. Read it, then reflect on verse 1:

> *Have mercy on me, O God, according to Your steadfast love; according to Your abundant mercy blot out my transgressions.*

Think about where you are right now in your life. What does this verse say to you?

Every spot-removal Web site begins with advice to first blot up as much of the stain as possible. David's word for "**blot**," *machah,* contains much of the same meaning as ours does: "to stroke or to rub, by implication to erase." But then it goes further: "to touch, i.e., reach to and utterly wipe away." His prayer, then, is for God to act according to His loving nature, to reach down and touch the area marred by sin, and to completely wipe it clean.

David continues, "Wash me thoroughly from my iniquity, and cleanse me from my sin!" (v. 2). Oh, the intrigue that was mine as I delved into the meaning of the word **cleanse**! In Hebrew, it is *kabac*, and it means first of all "to trample." *Is David asking God to trample him?* I wondered. Looking further, I saw that it also means "to wash by stamping with the feet, including the fulling process." Now that was a new one for me. "Fulling" is a process in fabric making, and you may have done it at home without even realizing it. Fulling is done by treating a fabric with hot water, heavy agitation, and soap. Heat, water, and agitation together cause the fibers to open up, lock together, and shrink. (Have you accidently put a sweater in a hot washer, only to find, when the cycle was complete, that it now would fit your chihuahua? *That* is "fulling"!)

The shrunken result of the fulling process is a fabric that is dense, durable, and irreversible. The process eliminates dirt, oil, and other impurities and makes the cloth thicker and stronger.

In asking God to wash him, David recognized that sometimes washing involves harsh processes. But it is only through God and the processes He puts us through that we can be cleaned— and we will come out of the process stronger than before.

5. "For I **know** my transgressions, and my sin is ever before me" (v. 3, emphasis added). The Hebrew word here is *yada* (yes, *that* word, made popular in conversational English by comedian Jerry Seinfeld). This word is used more than eight hundred times in the Old Testament, fifty-two times in Genesis alone. Look up the following passages to get a deeper understanding of what it means to "know" your transgressions. *Yada* has a differ-

ent connotation in each of the following verses. Can you create a synonym for how it is used? (Your translation may, in fact, use a different word.)

a. Genesis 3:7

b. Genesis 4:1

c. Genesis 12:11

d. Genesis 15:13

e. Genesis 24:21

f. Genesis 39:6

In Psalm 139, David is asking God to search for hidden sins, sins that he isn't aware of (like the spot of mustard on a colorful tie). Psalm 51, however, is concerned with sin that we are fully aware of—the gravy boat that dumped all down the shirt. Some of these are sins we've been living with for awhile; they have become familiar friends. My mother and conventional wisdom say that it's best to treat a stain right away; once it's been there for awhile, it is harder to get out. And if a stain has gone through the dryer, it will be nearly impossible to remove. The sins described in Psalm 51 have not only had a chance to set, but they've gone through the dryer several times. David says, in effect, "I've seen them with my own eyes; I know for certain they are sins, I've watched them closely, and I'm intimate with these sins."

6. Now that he's seen the sin, he asks God to treat it. "Cleanse me with hyssop, and I will be clean; wash me, and I will be whiter than snow" (v. 7, NIV). Read the following verses to see how hyssop was used in the Bible.

a. Exodus 12:22

b. Leviticus 14:2–7

c. Leviticus 14:49–53

d. Numbers 19:17–21

e. Hebrews 9:19–22

So hyssop was an element of the Passover, when the Jewish people were released from their bondage in Egypt. And it was part of Old Testament ritual cleansing before what had once been unclean could be pronounced clean. In the Book of Hebrews, however, we see that those ritual cleansings had to be repeated. But Christ was offered as a sacrifice "once for all" (Hebrews 10:10). "For by a single offering He has perfected for all time those who are being sanctified" (v. 14).

David says, "Wash me and I will be whiter than snow." Snow is a symbol of whiteness and purity. Procter and Gamble even named their laundry soap after it more than a hundred years ago—Ivory Snow—and used as its slogan "99 and 44/100ths percent pure." What image were they hoping to convey? That their soap would get your clothes as white as possible, as white as new snow. But David knew that when he asked God to wash him (literally to "un-sin him"), he would be so pure that there would be no figurative word to describe it.

7. The same imagery is used in Isaiah 1:18. What does God say here?

Although my chemical cocktail was useful in cleaning my crayon stains, no amount of effort on my part will clean my spiritual wash. Ritual cleansing comes with hyssop, used by the Israelites to sprinkle the blood of the lamb over their doorposts. True cleansing comes by the blood of the Lamb that covers my life.

8. No matter what our past contains, no matter how beyond redemption we appear, what does Paul tell us in 1 Corinthians 6:11?

When Paul uses the word **wash,** he uses *apolouo*, which means "to wash fully." There is a different Greek word that describes the cleansing of only a part of something. Similar in thought is the word *baptizo*, from which we get the word *baptism*. The root of this word was originally used in association with fabric dyeing, in which fabric was immersed in the dye and left there long enough to absorb the new color. When it was removed from the color, the fabric had a permanently changed appearance.

9. a. What does Romans 6:4 tell us happens in Baptism?

It's not the water only; it's the water and the Word, and our faith, which relies on the Word of God connected with the water, the washing of new life in the Holy Spirit. Baptism shows outwardly what God does inwardly. Baptism has permanent results.

Remember the fulling process discussed earlier? The cleansing process with water, heavy agitation, and soap eliminated oil, dirt, and other impurities. Why was this so important? Because oils and grease inhibit the binding action of dyes. Dye can't stick when oil and grease are there.

It's in this simple, completed action of Baptism in the water and the Word that God works forgiveness of sins, deliverance from death, and salvation for all who believe in Jesus Christ.

I am reminded of the Old Testament story of Naaman (2 Kings 5:1–14). Naaman, a powerful army commander, also had leprosy. When he was told that the prophet Elisha could cure him of his leprosy, he paid Elisha a visit. The prophet sent a servant to Naaman, telling him to go wash in the Jordan River seven times and his flesh would be restored and he would be clean. But Naaman wanted something more dramatic, more showy. In his anger at the simplicity, he almost missed the blessing.

When we are washed in the waters of Baptism, we are made clean. (It's interesting that someone healed from leprosy was also "made clean.") It is that profound and that simple. All the work is done by God—we just need to receive the new life.

b. According to 2 Corinthians 5:17, what happens when we are in Christ?

10. Unlike the unending chore of laundry, getting the spots out of our spiritual life isn't something we need to work on over and over. It was done once and for all when Jesus took our soiled and stained life to the cross. What are we told in Revelation 7:14?

My purple crayon experience gave laundry a new significance in my life. Now, instead of just seeing it as an automatic activity—something I do while I'm doing something else—I use it as an opportunity to review my day, to search for spots that need treating, to check for crayons hidden in the pockets of my life before they ruin my whole wardrobe, to confess those sins, and to seek deep spiritual cleansing from the only One who can make me spot free. Now *that's* a great way to spend a day!

As I pull the last load from the dryer and pair the last socks, I can finish with some words from David as well: "Let me hear joy and gladness; let the bones that You have broken rejoice. . . . Restore to me the joy of Your salvation, and uphold me with a willing spirit" (Psalm 51:8, 12).

And here's a fun word to complete our laundry analogy: the word **rejoice** used here is *guwl*—properly, it means "to spin around." While my clothes are spinning around in the dryer, I can spin around too, rejoicing in the freedom that comes from repentance and forgiveness.

11. How does Isaiah use a similar clean clothes analogy in Isaiah 61:10? (Note that the word translated "exult" in ESV is *guwl*.)

pest control
getting rid of spiritual bugs

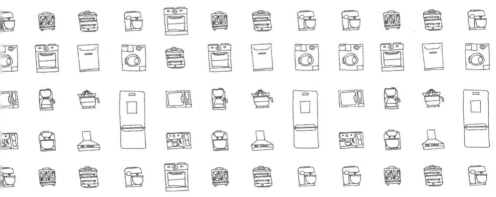

My earliest memory of insect infestation is from high school. We had flying ants in our family room that were about the size of wasps. When I heard those winged creatures land with a thud on a window, I would flee to a different room, abandoning whatever I was doing. I knew they couldn't really hurt me with a bite or a sting, but I disliked them nonetheless.

When I moved to my first apartment after college, there were roaches in the kitchen, not so much because I was a bad housekeeper (although I was), but because the old building was overrun with them. I refused to go in the kitchen after dark (which was probably good for my waistline) because I didn't want to see them scatter.

Another infestation came about six months after I was married. One day, I discovered tiny sugar ants all over the laundry basket in my bedroom closet. I looked everywhere to see where they were coming from, but I found no source. Then I remembered that I'd gathered laundry from my husband's closet as well. I looked there again and saw hundreds—thousands—of ants scurrying around a still-packed box. I quickly left the room, closed the door (the best way I know to avoid a problem), and called my husband. (Yes, I'm a wimp.) His search led him to a box of conversation hearts one of his students had given him at Valentine's Day, the week we got married. It got packed with his books, was buried in the back of the closet, and was forgotten. Although the candy box was still sealed, it was about half empty. Those tiny ants had been entering the box and devouring the sugar, then telling all their little ant friends about the sweet smorgasbord. While they were amassing their ant army, we were blissfully unaware.

Fifteen years later, tiny pests still torment me. Fire ant mounds pop up in our lawn seemingly overnight and swarm with creatures ready to attack my unclad feet. Microscopic ants also inhabit the space between my walls, moving between kitchen and bathrooms along pipes or electrical conduits. The exterminator tells me they are nearly impossible to destroy. We put out bait that attracts and then temporarily eliminates them, but we cannot find a solution that works permanently. I tell myself I'll have to learn to live with them, but still they bother me. What am I to do with pests I can't control?

What about you? What plagues you? If you have pets, your pest may be fleas. If you have a garden, your pests may be rabbits or deer or squash bugs. We all deal with pests of one type or another.

We also deal with persistent spiritual pests. Two of the most common I have found are fear and doubt. Like the Canaanites, Moabites, Edomites, and Ammonites, these parasites invade our territory, God's territory, whenever we turn around. Fear tries to divert us from fulfilling God's calling in our lives and causes us to focus on ourselves. Doubt causes us to question the concrete truths in Scripture, causes us to hear the world's view instead of the biblical view. And just when we think we've conquered them in one territory, they attack us in another. How annoying!

Let's look at some of the pests that plagued our biblical friends and that Satan still uses today to confuse us about God's will and the truth of His Word.

BiBLe STUDY QUeSTiONS

Moses

1. a. God calls Moses to lead His people out of Egypt in Exodus 3:10. What are four excuses Moses uses for not serving God in this capacity? (See vv. 11, 13; 4:1, 10.)

Earlier in his life, Moses had tried to relieve the suffering of his people to no avail (Exodus 2:11–16). The experience only left him fleeing to the desert. Now a flea of doubt that he could be of any use to God has gotten under his skin. Moses is filled with these doubts—doubts that he is skilled enough to do what God is asking him to do; doubts that anyone will listen; maybe even doubts about who God is. For each doubt, God has an answer. In each case, what is it?

b. Exodus 3:12

c. Exodus 3:14

d. Exodus 4:2–9

Spiritual Flyswatter

God assures Moses that He will go with him. He reminds Moses that He is the God of Abraham, Isaac, and Jacob; that He has a history with Moses and his people. When He calls Himself "I AM WHO I AM" (3:14), God is saying that He is the eternal, unchangeable, incomprehensible, and faithful God. This is the name by which God chose to be known and worshiped. When the Israelites call Him "Yahweh" (usually translated "the LORD"), they are saying "He is" or "He will be." *Yahweh* is the third-person form of the verb translated "I Am" (v. 14) and "I will be" (v. 12).

When we remember that God promises to go with us, that He has a history with us, and that He is the eternal, unchangeable, faithful God, we can swat away those flies that cause us to doubt our calling.

2. a. Moses' final plea with God is "Send someone else" (4:13). I've had this conversation with God; I imagine that almost everyone does. Think of a time when you had this same conversation with God. What was it about? What was the outcome?

I love that God already has a plan for this as well. In verse 14, we find out that Aaron is already on his way and that he can speak well. God didn't abandon the plan because of Moses' doubts, nor did He abandon Moses, leaving him to his fears. In God's plan, Moses and Aaron together became God's mouthpiece.

b. What are we told in Ecclesiastes 4:9–10? How does Jesus Himself send out His followers in Luke 10:1? Leaders in the Early Church followed the same practice (Acts 13:2).

c. Is there someone God has brought alongside you to help you serve Him and fill in the places where you are weak?

If not, perhaps you are being placed alongside someone else to help her serve. Who might that be, and how are you being called to serve?

d. Remember, too, that even when we are alone physically, we are not alone. Jesus gives another flyswatter just before He ascends into heaven. What does He say in Matthew 28:20?

Jeremiah

3. a. Jeremiah, too, had doubts when he was called by God. Read Jeremiah 1:4–10. What is Jeremiah's reply when God tells him He has appointed him as a prophet?

One morning several years ago, I awoke just *knowing* that I was to lead the women's retreat at our church the following year, even though I'd had no such thought when I went to bed. While I was sleeping, God gave me a theme, a theme song, and a plan for the retreat. I knew without a doubt that this was something the Holy Spirit was leading me to do, but the pest of self-doubt assailed me, and after attempting several other excuses (including Moses' "I'm not a good speaker"), I settled on one used by Jeremiah: "I'm too young to lead the retreat." God's response to me came less than a week later while I was at the grocery store. As I reached the checkout with my infant daughter, the cashier said to me, "Oh, shopping with your grandbaby today?" Ouch!

b. God's answer to me was as clear as His response to Jeremiah in verses 7–8. What was that response?

c. What similar words does God speak to Timothy through Paul in 1 Timothy 4:12?

Lest you think you are off the hook because you are "full in years," remember that Noah was six hundred years old when the floodgates opened (Genesis 7:11), Abram was seventy-five years old when God first called him (Genesis 12:4), and Moses was eighty when he first spoke to Pharaoh (Exodus 7:7).

Spiritual Flyswatter

4. Then, in words similar to those He said to Moses, what does God say in Jeremiah 1:9?

God would continue to put words in Jeremiah's mouth for more than forty years.

Gideon

5. a. In the time of the judges, Israel cried out to the Lord for deliverance, and God turned to Gideon to lead His people. Where was Gideon, and what was he doing when God called? (See Judges 6:11.)

The passage says he was trying to hide the wheat from the Midianites. While this could imply that Gideon was clever, it could also mean that he was simply scared and in hiding. After all, the Midianites were a deadly foe (see vv. 4–5), and Gideon felt abandoned by God (v. 13).

b. Gideon is facing a triple-pest threat: fear, futility, and forsakenness. What is his response to the Lord's calling? (See v. 15.)

c. Saul responds in a similar when he is told he will lead Israel (1 Samuel 9:21). In fact, when the time comes to show God's people who has been anointed their first king, where is Saul? (See 10:22.)

d. What about you? What pests do you face when called into God's service? Be honest. Do you hide, like Saul, behind the baggage of your past? behind a weak self-image? behind a family history that's less than glorious?

Spiritual Flyswatter

Like an old-time baseball umpire who just "calls 'em as he sees 'em," God calls us as He sees us, not as we see ourselves. He calls us "fearfully and wonderfully made" (Psalm 139:14), "holy and dearly loved" (Colossians 3:12 NIV), and "precious in [His] eyes" (Isaiah 43:4), even if this is not the way we see ourselves.

6. a. What does the angel of the Lord call Gideon when He appears to him? (See Judges 6:12.)

The Hebrew word for "man of valor" (or "mighty warrior," in NIV) is *chayil*. It means "a force." The angel is telling Gideon that he is a force to be reckoned with. The word also means "virtue, strength, power," and even "worthy." Certainly from his response so far, that's not how Gideon sees himself.

b. Have you, too, seen yourself as unworthy of God's calling? Look up Ephesians 2:10; then, rewrite the verse in your own words, and note here how they apply to your life right now.

God assures us that not only are we a work of art created in His image (Genesis 1:26), which He has said is "very good" (v. 31); but also that He has created us to do good works that He has prepared in advance for us to do. We also can have confidence in His promise that He will carry His work out to completion (Philippians 1:6). When we know that God's plan for us is good (Jeremiah 29:11), and we know He will be with us until the job is through, we only need to trust and obey.

c. When God calls, He also supplies. I love how this is stated in the second half of Isaiah 46:11 in the NIV: "What I have said, that will I bring about; what I have planned, that will I do." When Gideon says "I am weak," how does God respond? (See Judges 6:14, 16.)

d. The NIV text for verse 14 reads, "Go in the strength you have. . . . Am I not sending you?" In order for Gideon to see the strength God has supplied, he must begin to act in that strength. His first act is to tear down his father's altar to Baal. Gideon steps out to follow the Lord; but notice, when does he do this? (See v. 27.)

e. Baby steps in the right direction. Pest control. Soon God uses Gideon to defeat the Midianites in a way that shows God's mighty power. God reduced Gideon's forces from 32,000 men to just 300. What is the reason for this? (See 7:2.)

Talk about a fear factor! Sometimes God allows us to come up against an enemy that is so strong that we can do nothing but be afraid. Why would our loving Lord allow this to happen?

Because He knows that in the process, we will be drawn closer to Him and He will be glorified. Notice that before he goes into battle, Gideon bows down and worships God (v. 15). And in the end, Gideon and his tiny army of 300 leave 120,000 enemy swordsmen dead (8:10). Despite Gideon's feelings of fear, abandonment, and inadequacy, he is used mightily by God.

f. You can be too. Is there something to which God is calling you that seems too big or overwhelming to accomplish? Write it here. You need only "go in the strength you have" and remember that His power is made perfect in weakness (2 Corinthians 12:9).

David

7. No study of spiritual pests is complete until we talk about David. Although he faced every pest imaginable, we will focus on just one: Goliath. In fact, when Goliath sees David, he responds as if *he* were the one looking at a pest (1 Samuel 17:43). How easy it would have been for David to see himself as insignificant and inadequate, and to see the task as impossible—to be cowering in fear. After all, how have Saul and the Israelite soldiers responded to Goliath? (See v. 11.)

But that's not the story we hear of David. Instead, this teenage shepherd faces a truly incredible hulk named Goliath; and David is armed with only five smooth stones.

Spiritual Flyswatter

8. Okay, your turn: how does David overcome the swarm of fears that has overtaken an army so much more qualified than he? Read the whole story if you have time (1 Samuel 17:1–50), then concentrate on the following verses:

a. verse 26

b. verse 37

c. verse 45

In the ancient world, a name was not merely a label, but the meaning of the name was equivalent to the character of whoever bore it. The name of the Lord, then, is the manifestation of His character. Yahweh—God's personal, proper name—means "I AM," to be, exists, to cause to exist. The same God who revealed Himself to Moses in Exodus 3:13–14 is the God on whom David is calling.

d. And so, while everyone else is cowering in fear, while other mighty warriors have run away, what does the shepherd boy do? (See 1 Samuel 17:48–49.)

e. And for one final flyswatter, what do the following verses have in common? (You'll actually only need to read the first several words of each verse.)

1 Samuel 23:4

1 Samuel 30:8

2 Samuel 2:1

2 Samuel 5:19

2 Samuel 5:23

9. Summarize the flyswatters you've picked up in our study of

Moses, Jeremiah, Gideon, and David. How can you use them when facing your own spiritual pests?

Reviewing the lives of our Old Testament friends and seeing how God was faithful to bring His purposes to completion despite their fears and doubts, encourages and strengthens our faith. But ultimately, whether we do what God has called us to or run from it like Jonah did, our salvation rests not in our works, but in the work Christ already did for us on the cross. "For by grace you have been saved through faith. And this is not your own doing; it is the gift of God, not a result of works, so that no one may boast" (Ephesians 2:8–9). And that, my friend, is the best way I know of to get rid of those spiritual pests!

I'm happy to say that in the course of writing this lesson, I've dealt with some pest control issues of the insect kind. And since my husband was out of town, I didn't even leave the dead bugs on the floor for him to get rid of. (I used the vacuum cleaner to suck up those really big tree roaches you see in the South.) Now I just need to pick up my spiritual flyswatter and deal with my fears and doubts as well.

CLEANING OUT THE CLOSETS
WHAT NOT TO WEAR

Before you begin:
How are you at throwing stuff out?
What's the most cluttered room in your house?

Cleaning out the closets . . . or the garage . . . or the toy bin . . . All these tasks are daunting to me. So much stuff! What do I keep and what do I throw away? When my son was about four years old and Christmas was approaching, I decided to get rid of some old broken toys the kids didn't play with to make way for the new ones they would receive as Christmas gifts. I threw the toys into the garbage, expecting my husband to take the trash out before the kids got up. But of course, *that* morning, Matt woke up earlier than usual. Within a few minutes, for some unexplainable reason (broken-toy radar?), he went right to the trash can and peered in.

I have no words for the scene that ensued. It lasted all morning. Finally, distracted by Daddy, Matt calmed down. But when he saw the garbage truck on a nearby street, the scene began again.

Let me explain that the toys in the trash can were not expensive or really neat or favorites he couldn't bear to part with. This was just a tiny beach ball that no longer held air, part of a broken toy from a children's meal that some other child had left at the fast-food restaurant, and a few other broken pieces. Yet, Matt wanted to cling to them all.

Matt comes by this attachment honestly because I do the same kind of thing. One look at my clothes closet shows two things: (a) I have way too many clothes, and (b) I have *nothing* to wear. *How can this be?* I ask. When I look more closely, I see clothes that no longer fit well, are out of style, or have no match; I see clothes that I bought because the styles were cute on someone else or on the hanger (but not on me); and I see clothes that have tears, stains, or broken zippers. Yet I cannot seem to throw any of them away or give them to someone who would find them more useful.

I've often watched a show on cable TV that intrigues me. Family and friends of a "fashion faux pas" (FFP) turn in their friend to the "fashion police" for a total makeover. The fashion police point out the flaws in her wardrobe choices and teach her what looks good on her. After her lesson, she is sent on a big-city shopping spree with a prepaid credit card while they watch her pick out a new wardrobe.

What fascinates me is that in every show, the FFP first buys clothes that resemble the old her, the things she's been comfortable in for so long. Although she has been shown how unbecoming they are on her and has been told exactly what styles to look for to complement her body type, it's as if the old, unbecoming styles jump right off the rack and into her arms.

I have a lot in common with the FFP. And it's not just the unattractive clothes in my closet. It's that her chronic shopping problems resemble my approach to my own spiritual life. Maybe you can relate to this problem I share with Israel's first king, Saul, as well. Let's take a trip to 1 Samuel and look in Saul's closet.

BiBLe STUDY QUESTiONS

1. a. As the period of the judges was ending in Israel and Samuel was growing old, the people began asking for a king. While Samuel saw this as a personal rejection, God had a different perspective. What was it? (See 1 Samuel 8:7–9.)

b. The concept of a king for Israel was not a new idea from God; He had anticipated a king for Israel already in Genesis 49:10 and built it into His redemption plan. However, the motive behind the people's desire for a king was the problem. What were Israel's motives, according to 1 Samuel 8:19–20?

c. So God says, "Obey their voice and make them a king" (v. 22). And Saul enters the picture. What do you learn about Saul and his background from 9:1–2?

When we learn that his father, Kish, is "a man of wealth," the Hebrew words here tell us that he was powerful, a warrior, a champion. Kish was impressive, and his son, Saul, was spoken of in physically glowing terms.

d. When Kish's donkeys get lost, Saul and a servant are sent on a wild donkey chase, but they are unable to catch up with the beasts. Verses 5–7 give some insight into Saul's character. From these verses, what type of person can you infer that Saul is? Give evidence to support your statements.

God had already revealed to Samuel that he would anoint a Benjamite to be the king Israel begged for (vv. 15–16). When Saul approaches the prophet Samuel, Samuel reveals something far bigger than lost donkeys. He tells Saul that "all that is desirable in Israel" (v. 20) is turned toward Saul and his family. "All that is desirable in Israel" is code language for Israel's desire for a king, so Samuel has, in fact, revealed to Saul that he has been chosen to be the king of Israel.

2. a. What is Saul's response (v. 21)?

b. Do you know someone like Saul? someone who, from outward appearances, has it all—good looks, social standing, a good family, and so forth—but has a very low opinion of the person in the mirror? (Remember that 1 Samuel 9:1 tells us about Saul's family; v. 21 is just how Saul sees himself.)

3. a. Samuel then does an extraordinary thing. He invites Saul over for dinner. (No, that's not the extraordinary part—that's just hospitality.) Describe the dinner. (See vv. 22–24.)

b. When Samuel gave Saul the leg (literally, the thigh), he wasn't just giving him a serving of meat—he was making a statement. To whom is the thigh offered according to Leviticus 7:32–34?

Samuel is setting Saul apart, giving him a distinct honor reserved for God's anointed ones, the priests. Until that time, only the priests were anointed. But beginning with Saul, and from this time forward in the Old Testament, it is the king who is referred to as "the anointed one of the Lord." The anointing occurs in 1 Samuel 10:1.

A bit like an inauguration or a swearing in to office but without the pomp (anointing was probably a private affair that preceded the public announcement), anointing signifies a setting apart to the Lord for a particular task *and* a divine equipping for the task.

In verses 2–7, Samuel explains to Saul the signs God will send that will authenticate his words and assure Saul that God has indeed chosen him as king.

c. Read verses 2–7. What are the three signs?

d. Now focus on verses 6–7. The New Testament disciples were told the same thing. What does Jesus tell them in Acts 1:8?

"You will receive **power**" (Acts 1:8). In Greek, it's *dunamis*. The noun comes from the verb, which means "to be able." It means "force, ability, abundance, might, power." In a nutshell, when they receive the Spirit, they receive His power. The same is said to Saul.

In 1 Samuel 10:9, we read that "God gave [Saul] another **heart**." The Hebrew word is *leb*, and it means not just "heart," but also "the feelings," "the will," and even "the intellect." This is Saul's makeover; God changes him from the inside out. All the signs Samuel prophesied were fulfilled that day.

4. a. What evidence is there that Saul has changed? (See vv. 10–11.)

b. But there's also evidence that despite his change, despite the promise of verse 6, Saul is still returning to the same clothes he used to wear as he puts on the same old self. Read verses 14–27 to find this evidence. Even the last sentence of the chapter reflects on Saul's character. Describe what happened and what it might indicate about Saul.

Saul's early kingship is rewarded with early victories. When the Ammonites threaten to "gouge out . . . [the] right eyes" of everyone in Jabesh Gilead (11:2), "the Spirit of God rushed upon

Saul . . . and his anger was greatly kindled" (v. 6). Saul and his men soundly defeated the Ammonites (v. 11), and the people confirmed him as their king (vv. 12–15).

5. a. To whom does Saul give credit for this victory? (See v. 13.)

b. 1 Samuel 12 is Samuel's retirement speech. What is his final piece of professional advice for the Israelites, who no longer have a need for a judge now that they have a king? (See vv. 24–25.)

As 1 Samuel 13 begins, Saul is in the second year of his reign. These verses give us a glimpse back into the wardrobe of a man whose clothes don't fit. Saul chooses an army of three thousand men, keeping two thousand and sending a thousand with his son, Jonathan. The rest of the people he sends back home. Then Jonathan attacks the Philistine outpost.

6. a. When Saul sounds the trumpet to announce what has happened, what is the word on the street concerning Israel (v. 4)?

b. Why might he have expected them to react differently? (Think back to 11:12 in question 5.)

c. Vastly outnumbered, how do the Israelites react? (See 13:5–7.)

d. What does this tell you about Saul's character and leadership?

e. In fact, years later, David will face an equally outsized enemy with an entirely different attitude. Read his prayer in Psalm 3:1–8. How does his reaction differ from Saul's? What do you think accounts for the difference in attitude toward a formidable enemy in these two men?

Now read 1 Samuel 13:8–15. It may be painful to watch as Saul pulls one thing after another out of the closet, trying to find something that works. (Admittedly, this whole metaphor would work better if Saul were a woman, since my husband, at least, rarely tries more than one outfit to see what works. I, on the other hand . . .)

7. a. Verse 8 tells us "he **waited** seven days." The Hebrew is *yachal*. It means "to wait, to be patient, to hope, to trust." What is it that Saul waited for? To better understand, return to 10:8.

b. Can you relate to Saul's "wardrobe malfunction"? Have you waited patiently on the Lord to a point, but then given up because God was taking too long? Have you hoped and trusted in God right up until the time He didn't seem to come through for you? Impatience is one article of clothing I frequently pull from my closet. How about you? Think about a time in your life (maybe right now) when it seemed that God was taking a long time to answer your prayer. How did you respond? What was the eventual outcome?

c. Remember that God promises to always hear our prayers (1 John 5:14), and He assures us that whatever we ask that is according to His will will be done (v. 15). Notice, too, Jesus' reminder in Matthew 10:29–31. What is that reminder?

d. God does indeed see you and hear your prayers. He cares for you (1 Peter 5:7), so you can give all your fears and anxieties to Him. How does this knowledge prepare you for the next time you have a wardrobe malfunction?

e. In what other ways does Saul make errors in judgment in 1 Samuel 13:8–15? Make your own list here:

I'm tempted to let Saul off the hook because I sympathize with him. I also try to make my own excuses when I pull something out of my own closet that isn't right, like the shirt with a spot. (Maybe I could say I just got the spot on it that morning and didn't have time to change, or I could claim that I didn't notice the stain until I was out of the house.) I want to say that perhaps Saul forgot what Samuel had said in 1 Samuel 10:8. I want to deny that he caused the problem in the first place. Yet I know that Samuel clearly told Saul to go to Gilgal and wait, and Saul went against that by sending Jonathan to the outpost. Now the mistakes are compounded. Saul offers up the sacrifice (Leviticus 3:1–5 makes it clear that this offering is to be made by the priests only). Then, in 1 Samuel 13:11, Saul passes the buck: "You didn't come when you said you were going to come. The Philistines were getting ready to attack us, so I had to do something," he says in desperation. Have you pulled this out of your closet as well? Never mind that the Philistines were attacking only because Saul had attacked first, without God's permission.

f. In verse 12, he plays the religion card: "I hadn't sought God's favor, so *I* had to offer a sacrifice." The KJV says, "I forced myself." Have you jumped into something with both feet before realizing you were in over your head, then gone to God to ask for His favor? Tell about the situation here if you'd like, and the outcome:

So what is it? Did Saul want God's blessing, or did he find himself forced to ask for God's blessing? Either way, he's digging a deeper hole for himself. Perhaps this shy man with low self-esteem began to believe his own PR, or he was overcompensating for his own self-doubt. Perhaps he was playing the role as he thought a king would play it, lest his people begin to suspect their emperor had no clothes. Perhaps he forgot that his initial victory in battle came not because he was such a great leader, but because "the Spirit of God rushed upon [him]" (11:6). Whatever the reason, Saul has forgotten that he has been changed, and he returns to his old wardrobe—a choice that costs him dearly.

8. a. Remember, Samuel had laid out the new wardrobe in 12:24. Need a refresher? Write the words here again:

b. What is the price Saul pays? (See 13:13–14.)

Saul's other ugly wardrobe choices are apparent throughout the Book of 1 Samuel, so I won't belabor the point. Besides, the point is not just about Saul; it's about you and me.

9. a. We, too, have been given a makeover in Christ. What are Paul's words in 2 Corinthians 5:17?

Yet I hang on to what's in my closet. Paul pleads with me to throw the old away and put on the new. Read Colossians 3:1–5.

Like the fashionistas telling the FFP "Here's what to shop for, here's what looks good on you," Paul says, **"Set your minds on things that are above"** (v. 2). The Greek word is *phroneo*, and it means "to exercise the mind, to entertain, interest oneself, regard, savor." I'm guilty of shopping for clothes and walking right by a rack, saying, "That would never look good on me," only to find out it was perfect for my frame. The same can be said for trying things God's way. Is there something you've been afraid to try because you thought it would never work on you? Maybe there's no room for it in a closet filled with an old wardrobe. Maybe it's time to clean out your closet.

b. What habits or attitudes would you like to get rid of?

c. Paul's words toward our old attitudes and habits are pretty strong. What should we do with our "old wardrobe" (or, as Paul calls it, "what is earthly in [us]," v. 5)?

The wardrobe imagery is a nice metaphor to use as we consider this whole transformation, but it didn't originate with me. In fact, Paul's original language in Colossians suggests it. The words of verses 9–10 "put off the old self with its practices and . . . put on the new self" are clothing words. The Greek word used here for **put off** is *apekduomai,* and it translates "to strip, to take off, to unclothe."

Where we say **put on the new self**, Paul says *enduo,* which translates "sinking into a garment; to invest with clothing." How do you relate to that imagery? What kind of picture does it bring to mind? It's vivid to me. This garment I can sink into sounds especially comfortable. It's also something I invest in, something that says quality and expense. In fact, this new wardrobe is both expensive and free. It was bought with a price (1 Corinthians 7:23) too costly for us to pay.

10. a. What is the cost, according to 1 Peter 1:18–19?

Our new wardrobe is bought and paid for by the blood of the Lamb, by Jesus' willingness to lay down His own life so that we might have life, to suffer under the weight of sin because it was a burden too heavy for us to bear. And yet, the cost was borne entirely by Him and is of no cost to us. Romans 6:23 tells us that the free gift of God is eternal life in Christ Jesus.

b. What are we told in Galatians 3:27?

c. **"Put on"** is *enduo* again. When we are baptized into Christ, we put on His garments, and they are rich indeed, clothes ready for a celebration. Read Isaiah 61:10. I'm ready to get decked out. How about you? Write your thoughts here:

Finally, as the metaphor concludes, the new clothes I'm putting on—"the new self," as Paul calls it (Colossians 3:10)—are being **renewed**. The Greek word here, *anakainoo,* means "renovated, a freshness, a reversal." And who is the Designer? The One who designed me in the first place, my Creator. Refresh your memory by reading Genesis 1:27.

God created each of us in His image, and now He's reversing the process that sin has worked on us. He is restoring us into His **image** ("likeness, resemblance").

d. As you clean out the closet to make room for your new wardrobe, don't forget the one accessory that Paul says makes the whole outfit—any outfit—complete. Read Colossians 3:14; what is it?

And who among us doesn't like a little accessorizing? Enjoy your new wardrobe!

MRS. FIX-IT
A LESSON IN REBUILDING

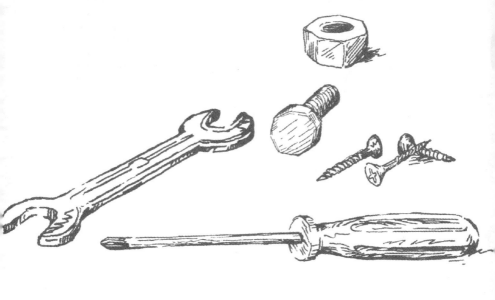

*When it comes to home repairs, are you more likely to do it your-
self, hire out, or let the damage get worse while you try to make
a decision, really hoping the problem will go away?*

I'm not exactly handy with a toolbox. My husband and I aren't
Mr. and Mrs. Fix-it. In fact, we tend to ignore a repair as long
as possible. Here's an example: For more than a year we had
a fence picket just inside or outside our garage door—not
because we had a hole in the fence, but because we used it to
prop up our garage door whenever we opened it, lest it come
crashing down on our heads as we got the bikes or other toys
in and out of the garage.

We have a hole in the linoleum of our kitchen floor. It's not in
a corner where it goes unnoticed, but right smack-dab in the
middle of the path where we enter the kitchen and walk between the cooking area and the eating area. It measures about
12 inches by 2 inches now—although it started as a tiny buckle
that probably could have been fixed with a twopenny nail. Now
we need to replace the entire floor.

We just are not repairers.

And it's not just house projects, so I can't blame my husband.
I'm a seamstress, but I don't mend. I'd much rather make a garment from scratch than fix a zipper or replace a hem. One day,
my daughter, a confirmed clothes-aholic, came into the sewing
room and looked in the closet. "Are those clothes for me?" she
asked, pointing at two folded items high on the closet shelf.
"No," I said, "they're for Daddy and me. They need fixing."
Then it occurred to me that they've been waiting to be fixed

for at least nine years. They found their way to that place in the closet when we moved the sewing room to make room for the arrival of our son. There they were, still on a shelf, still waiting for buttons to be replaced. Like I said, I'm just not a fixer.

At times, I tell myself, *That's just not who I am, who God created me to be.* Other times, I think, *I wish I could do that, but I'm too afraid of making a mistake to even give it a try.* Sometimes I think it's too much work; then I throw my hands up in despair, saying I don't have the time.

Yes, our "stuff" needs mending, but I've realized time and again that relationships are often in need of mending as well. As often as I am reminded of Jesus' command to "love one another," I may quit on a relationship, put it on a high shelf, or let a situation go on so long that a tiny tear of misunderstanding becomes a gaping hole in the fabric of the relationship, and it seems that what is done cannot be undone. I like to avoid conflict and hide my head in the sand, so it seems that I have forgotten Jesus' words: "In this world you will have trouble. But take heart! I have overcome the world" (John 16:33 NIV).

BiBLe STUDY QUeSTiONS

1. a. My inclination is to sit by and hope that whatever needs repairing will heal itself. But God reminds me that when it comes to my faith life, I am not to just sit idly by, but to participate in the rebuilding/repairing process. One such reminder is in Isaiah 58:12. Describe what the words to this passage mean to you.

It's not just homes that need repairing, but relationships as well. In fact, one word in the Old Testament, *bayith*, is translated in the NIV Bible as **"wall"** (Ezekiel 40:43), **"family"** (Genesis 7:1), and **"household"** (Genesis 17:27).

In Isaiah 58:12, "repairer of the breach" can also be translated "Repairer of Broken Walls" (NIV). The Hebrew word is *perets*, and it means "gap." A standard dictionary may also include these meanings for *breach*: something that results from a break or rupture, a severance of friendly relations, or even a wound.

b. How does your dictionary define *breach*?

The same Hebrew phrase used in Isaiah 58:12 and translated "Repairer of Broken Walls" or "repairer of the breach" is translated differently in Ezekiel 22:30: "who would **build up** the wall and stand before me in **the gap**" (NIV).

2. a. Whom does the Lord say He found to "stand in the gap" according to verse 30?

b. According to verse 31, what will be the result?

That's kind of a shocking statement from God: "I looked for someone to stand in the gap and I found none." Using the same word from the Isaiah passage, that verse could read, "I looked for someone to repair the wall, but I found no one."

c. Psalm 106 has a picture of "gap standing." Read verses 19–23. According to verse 21, what—or whom—had the people

(Israel) forgotten?

d. So what would God have done? (See v. 23.)

e. What did Moses do?

Moses stood in the gap and prayed for God's mercy and favor
for the children of Israel. We are called by God to do the same,
to be "repairers of the wall" in our own homes and neighbor-
hoods, within our families and other relationships. There are
gaps to be breached within the walls of our relationships.

Today, psychologists urge us not to put up walls in our relationships since walls are seen as divisions and barriers. Yet somehow, we seem to have learned that "good fences make good
neighbors," and we feel that it's better to have walls that isolate
us from one another. However, in the ancient world, walls were
always seen as protection and fortification, and being inside
the city walls was the safest place to be. Rather than signifying
isolation, walls offered protection for all who dwelled together
within them. That is precisely what families, friendships, and
close relationships were designed to be: our sanctuary, our safe
place.

But what happens when there is a breach in the wall of security
of our family? What do we do when there's "severance of friendly relations" or "stepping across a boundary"? Maybe there is
alienation, a split, rift, schism, or dissension—all synonyms for
breach. And remember, a breach can also be a wound. Maybe
there's a wound right within our own homes that needs healing.

f. Now it's time to be honest. In the space below, identify a breached wall that needs rebuilding in your life. It might be a strained relationship with a spouse, the alienation of a child, some dissension with your mother-in-law, a friendship that seems to be distant. Use code language if you have to, but write it here. If you truly cannot think of any broken relationships in which you are involved, your job in this lesson is to pray diligently for those who find themselves in the midst of such a painful gap.

So what exactly does it mean to be a "Repairer of Broken Walls," a repairer of the breach, and how do we do it? We have a biblical model in the prophet Nehemiah, who can be considered the Old Testament rebuilder of walls in Jerusalem. He tells us that he is the cupbearer to the king (Nehemiah 1:11). The cupbearer, among other duties, was the king's official food taster, making sure his food wasn't poisoned—a person my husband says is fully dependable and fully expendable. Nehemiah wasn't a trained wall builder, psychologist, or family counselor, and neither are most of us. But he *was* the king's servant, and as Christians, so are we. Put yourself, then, in Nehemiah's position as we learn to rebuild the walls.

3. a. **Step 1:** Read Nehemiah 1:1–7. What did Nehemiah learn had happened to the wall of Jerusalem?

b. What is his response?

c. Notice that after weeping, mourning, and fasting, Nehemiah begins his prayer with adoration (he calls God "great and awesome," v. 5), then moves to confession. Write the words of confession that Nehemiah uses here:

The model to begin repairing breaches is clear: begin by acknowledging the awesomeness of God and the sin of mankind, and our own sin in particular. Notice, too, that there is no blame shifting and no attempt to minimize the sin. (Recall similar words from David in Psalm 51:3–4.)

That's where *our* rebuilding efforts must begin as well: by coming before God in prayer and confession, and by coming to His presence in the Sacraments. It is here, in Holy Communion, where our Lord Jesus Christ restores and refreshes us with His body and blood. It is here that He bridges the breaches caused by our sin, even as we hear the words "This is My body . . . this is My blood, given and shed for you for the forgiveness of sins," and He restores us to God the Father.

d. In the space below, come to God with your confession. If this seems too public to you, write your response on a separate piece of paper, then burn it or shred it. But don't miss out on your part in this important step in rebuilding that broken relationship.

4. a. **Step 2:** Read Nehemiah 2:1–5. Describe Nehemiah's demeanor as he goes before the king:

b. We persist in difficult times because we fail to acknowledge our own sinful behaviors and thoughts. When we put on a brave front, telling ourselves that we can handle our problems on our own, we fail to acknowledge a problem for what it is—sin. But as one of my friends says, the elephant is still in the middle of the room and cannot be ignored. What is Nehemiah's immediate response to the king's question of verse 4 before he opens his mouth to reply?

"Whisper prayers," as they might be called, may last only a moment, but they help to make God's words your words. Only after praying does Nehemiah open his mouth to speak aloud. How often we would be blessed to follow his example!

c. Notice Nehemiah 2:10. How do Sanballat and Tobiah react to this request to rebuild?

Not everyone will applaud your attempt at reconciliation. Sanballat, whose Babylonian name means "Sin has given life," is an expected opposition to Nehemiah. He is a political opponent of Nehemiah's and does not want the walls rebuilt (4:1–2). However, Tobiah, whose name means "The LORD is good," is probably a worshiper of Yahweh, the Lord. His opposition is much less expected (v. 3). At times, then, even our Christian friends may not support us in rebuilding a relationship. Because we each have been marked by sin (Romans 3:23), each of us apart from Jesus Christ lives according to our sinful nature. Paul says, "I know that nothing good dwells in me, that is, in my flesh" (7:18). Blinded by sin, our friends and family might pursue their own agendas—or even think they have our best interests at heart.

Step 3: Read Nehemiah 2:11–18. With this passage, Nehemiah begins the process of examining the wall, inspecting the damage.

5. a. First, note what Nehemiah does *not* do. (See vv. 12, 16.)

The word "**told**" here is *nagad* and means "to manifest, to announce, expose, predict, explain." Today we might rather not call it gossip when we gather with a group of friends and assess a situation. My dictionary defines gossip this way: "idle talk or rumor, especially about the personal or private affairs of others." It's interesting to note where the word gossip originates. In Old English (before 1050 AD), the word was *God + sibbe*. *Sibbe* (or *sib*) means "related." If I look at the Old English definition, then, I can boil down gossip to "talking with one another when we should be talking with God."

b. What problems might have resulted if Nehemiah had gathered a group of people to discuss the wall damage in this early stage? Numbers 13:31–33 gives one example of this unhealthy kind of discussion, but there are other problems as well.

c. What problems can you foresee in the early stages of relationship rebuilding and reconciliation if you discuss them with a group of friends?

Jesus Himself gives instructions to not start working on a problem by telling a group, but instead, to take the direct approach and talk one-on-one. (See Matthew 18:15.)

d. Finish this sentence from Nehemiah 2:12: "And I told no one what _____."

e. This is important too. Rebuilding the wall is what God had put on Nehemiah's heart—that is, what He had "ascribed, assigned, or directed" to Nehemiah. We cannot begin to think we can rebuild a relationship if God isn't putting that task on our heart. In fact, what are God's words to us in Psalm 127:1?

Step 4: Read Nehemiah 2:17–18. After assessing the damage and listening to what God has put on his heart, Nehemiah does discuss what he has learned with those around him, laying out a plan, to which they reply, "Let's rebuild the walls!" Much of the rest of the Book of Nehemiah involves the events of rebuilding the walls.

6. a. **Step 5:** Read Nehemiah 2:19–20. How do Sanballat, Tobiah, and Geshem react when they hear about the rebuilding effort?

b. In the KJV, verse 19, the words used are "laughed us to scorn and despised us." Now read Luke 8:53, and see where a similar phrase appears; in fact, in the KJV, it is the same phrase. The words will be similar in your translation. What is the situation here?

Sometimes efforts to rebuild relationships will be met with derision: "they laughed us to scorn." Not everyone will have heard God speak to your heart to rebuild that relationship with a wayward spouse, an abusive parent, a rebellious child, a friend who broke a confidence. But just as Jesus was despised and ridiculed for saying the child was not dead, "but sleeping" (v. 52), and just as He raised her to new life, so He, through you, can breathe life back into a relationship.

c. What is Nehemiah's response to Sanballat and his friends? (See Nehemiah 2:20.)

Notice that he takes no credit for what is about to occur, but instead gives it all to the God of heaven. We would be wise to do the same.

7. a. **Step 6:** Read Nehemiah 4:7–23. The job doesn't get easy just because the rebuilding has begun. In fact, as rebuilding begins, plots are stirred up against it. How does Nehemiah respond in verse 9?

b. What is happening to the strength of the laborers (v. 10)?

c. How does Nehemiah respond (v. 13)?

I believe the comparison to relationship rebuilding is direct. Troubles will come. Satan will try to destroy the work that God has done to restore you to Him. Watch and pray. You will get tired. The task will seem hopeless and unending. Watch and pray. Notice that by this time, Nehemiah has called in others to keep watch with him and to pray with him. He didn't try to go it alone. He didn't call his friends in to gossip and discuss the situation, but rather to stand guard with him and pray with him.

8. Nehemiah doesn't let the distractions keep him from the task

of rebuilding, but he does make sure the laborers are properly armed against the enemy. To be properly prepared for our spiritual enemies, we must arm ourselves as well. Compare Nehemiah 4:16–18 with Ephesians 6:11–18. Note the differences or similarities here:

9. a. Finally, Nehemiah 4:14 directly addresses why we are rebuilding the walls. Write the quote from verse 14 in your own words here:

Our families and, by extension, our friends and relationships are worth fighting for. The walls of safety and security are worth rebuilding.

b. So often in the Old Testament, when God's people are faced with a daunting task or a challenge that seems impossible, God comes to them with words of hope. What words or phrases are the same in Deuteronomy 1:29–30; 3:22; 20:3–4; and Nehemiah 4:14?

Yes, the battle is not ours, but God's. We will fail if we try to stand alone, if we enter a battle that God hasn't appointed for us, or if we begin to think that we are able to save anyone. Salvation comes through Christ alone, not by our works; the real restorer of relationships is Jesus Christ, who reconciled all things to Himself, "making peace by the blood of His cross" (Colossians 1:20). Jesus makes it clear that we are to restore relationships with our brother or sister (Matthew 5:24) and that we cannot say we love God and yet hate our brother (1 John 4:20).

Like Nehemiah, when we see the walls in disrepair, a family relationship that is damaged, a friendship where gates have been burned, we must not sit idly by, but instead, seeking God's wisdom and plan, we take our part in the rebuilding, doing the work that God has prepared in advance for us to do (Ephesians 2:10).

10. Now, using the steps outlined in this lesson, what is the next step you will take in restoring that relationship you wrote about in 2f?

STocKing UP oN THE FRUiT oF THE SPiRiT,

PART 1

Before you begin:
How good are you at buying the "right foods"?
How good are you about eating the "right foods"?

I realized the orange juice didn't taste right as soon as I took a sip. Maybe it had been in the fridge too long. After all, I had been away for Christmas vacation for two weeks, and I had mixed it up from frozen concentrate some time before I left—I couldn't remember exactly when. So I dumped the glass and the rest from the container down the drain. When I went about the task of cleaning the container, something happened that I've never seen before. The inside of the plastic container melted when I rinsed it with hot water. Apparently the acid from the OJ had eaten away at the plastic. Yikes!

I had bought the juice with the best intentions, to get one serving of fruit with my breakfast. But it wasn't enough just to *buy* it—I had to *drink* it as well.

I confess I have left plastic containers of leftovers in my refrigerator until the foods they contained were unrecognizable. (Please, somebody, admit with me that you have done this too.) Rather than peek inside to see how badly the food has spoiled (I have a weak stomach and a sensitive nose), sometimes I just throw the food away, container and all.

Although my habits in the area of healthy diet have improved, I still "buy it but don't eat it" more often than I want to admit. Diet experts tell us we should have the good stuff (fruits and veggies) washed and cut in the fridge so they'll be ready and waiting, easy to grab when we're hungry. So off I go to the grocery store to stock up on what's fresh and healthy. Unfortunately, although food that's good for me is in my fridge, I find that junk food is easier to grab. Chips are still more appealing to me than carrots. What doesn't make sense is that when I resist temptation and choose healthy food over junk food, I know that it's better for me; I'm taking care of my physical health. Fruit and veggies are sweet and satisfying, and I just feel better when I eat them. Still, my "flesh is weak" (Matthew 26:41).

Interesting, isn't it, that the same can be said for my walk with Christ? Although I can confidently lay claim to "the good stuff," certain that Jesus came so that I may have life abundantly (John 10:10), too often the good stuff just sits there while I give in to the weakness of my flesh and turn instead to "junk food," the quick and easy, however unhealthy it is for my soul. And while God has made the good food available to me through Jesus Christ, He will not force me to eat it. In fact, He tells me through Moses that He has set before me life and death, blessings and curses, and He tells me to choose life (Deuteronomy 30:19).

BiBLe STUDY QUeSTiONS

1. a. Thoughts on the contents of my refrigerator lead me directly to thoughts on the fruit of the Spirit. Begin by reading Galatians 5:22–25, then list the fruit of the Spirit:

The English word **fruit** is derived from the Latin *fructus,* which means "enjoyment, profit, fruitful"—in other words, "to enjoy the produce of." Do you enjoy the produce of the Spirit? Or does the fruit remain untouched in your life, like the cauliflower, broccoli, and grapes in your crisper? Just as it sometimes seems more satisfying to grab the chips and the chocolate, so it is in our spiritual lives. We grab impatience because we think ourselves too important to wait; we pick up a harsh word rather than a kind one because we feel we've been wronged and that other person has it coming. Maybe (okay, no "maybe" about it) we need to stop praying for the fruit of the Spirit as if it were beyond our grasp or a wish we want to be granted.

b. What does God tell us in Deuteronomy 30:11–14 concerning His commands and His Word?

In Deuteronomy 30:14, the word "**word**" is *dabar.* Among its many definitions are "portion + power, promise and provision." God has provided us with everything we need. He's given us the portion we need, and He's given us the power to access it. It's time to start using the fruit the Holy Spirit has already placed in our heart.

2. a. So the first question is, have I stocked my refrigerator with the good stuff? Do I really have the Spirit in my heart? We find the answer in the words of Ephesians 1:13. Rewrite the verse in your own words here:

b. And again, to answer the question "Does the Spirit live in me?" what does God tell us through Peter in Acts 2:38?

"Repent and be baptized . . . and you **will** receive the gift of the Holy Spirit." The word *will* is the imperative auxiliary verb. For those of you who aren't grammar geeks, that's a "helper word" that helps to clarify the verb that follows it (in this case, "receive"). Here, the word "will" means "it's an absolute necessity, unavoidable." So in this passage, God, through Peter, tells us that when we are baptized into Jesus' name and repent of our sins, we receive forgiveness and the gift of the Holy Spirit. It's unavoidable. And when we receive the Holy Spirit, we receive His fruit. *Fruit* is a collective noun. It means we get the whole basket, not just a single piece; the bunch of grapes, not just a single one. We don't receive love and not joy, or patience and not self-control. And in Galatians 5:23, we read that "against such things there is no law." That means that we receive *all* of these things and receive them all without measure. There is no limit to the fruit of the Spirit! It comes to us in abundant measure.

3. a. So if we've got the assurance of forgiveness through Spirit-given faith, then why is it that we so often struggle with worry, impatience, a lack of self-control—responses that are the opposite of the fruit of the Spirit? Paul faced the same question in Romans 7:14–15. What does Paul say he is in verse 14?

Paul is saying, "I'm flesh and blood—I'm human." **Sold** under sin is *piprasko*, which means, "to traverse, to traffic, to travel." When I think of traffic, I think of all the cars on the freeway at rush hour—horns honking, tempers flaring, a tangled mess of cars where no one is making much progress. While there was no rush hour in ancient Greece, of course, I think this is an appropriate comparison. Think about it.

b. What connection can you make between your human nature and traffic?

Or think of traffic in the commercial sense: buying and selling of goods and services. It's difficult to think of this in any way but negatively, with the connotations of drug or human trafficking. And that's what Paul is talking about. We have sold ourselves to sin. In fact, we were born into sin (Psalm 51:5) and have spent our lives gratifying the desires of our sinful natures (Ephesians 2:3). In fact, that is where we are stuck without Jesus.

c. How does Paul expand the thought in Romans 7:19–20?

Try as we might, sin **dwells** within. The Greek word is *oikeo*, and it tells me that sin occupies the house and has moved in with the whole family. Yes, we know that the Holy Spirit lives in us, but so often our lives don't display the fruit of that Spirit. Praise God that our salvation is not dependent on how much effort we put into it or whether or not our actions follow. Jesus lived a perfect and sinless life in our place; there is hope for every believer in Christ.

d. Ephesians 2:3 ends with our carrying out the desires of our flesh, living by our sinful natures and opposed to God. But verses 4–5 begin in a different way: "But God . . . ." **But** is a conjunction (a joining word) that shows that what follows is an opposite. This was our condition *except* for God, *save* for God, *if not* for God, *without* God. How have things changed! What is our condition now *because of* God, who is rich in mercy?

e. What does Paul say in Romans 7:24–25?

In my sinfulness, I like to use the excuse that "I'm just not a patient person." Or I say, "God hasn't given me the fruit of self-control yet. I guess I'll just have to keep praying for it." In reality, if the Spirit dwells inside me (and He does!), then I also have access to His fruit, *all* of it, and in unlimited supply. So it's time for a little more word etymology. Hold on to your hats!

The Greek word for **fruit** is *karpos*, which is from the base of *harpazo*, which means "to seize, pluck, take by force." *Harpazo* is derived from *haireomai* (you'll just have to trust me on this, unless you're a scholar of ancient languages, just as I trust my *Strong's Concordance of the Bible*). *Haireomai* means "to take for oneself, i.e., to prefer, to choose." Follow the chain with me: you can live by your sinful nature, or you can **choose** to live by the Spirit.

4. All this is, of course, after we have been chosen through the work of the Spirit when we were baptized. Write the words to John 15:16 here:

God wants His followers to **bear fruit**, which means to bring forth or be driven. Jesus says that He wants us to be driven by our fruit, for the fruit of the Holy Spirit to be the driving force in our lives. (See John 15:8.) Let's take a closer look at the fruit in our basket.

The first fruit on the list is **love**. You may be aware of the three words for "love" used in the New Testament. The first is *eros*—that's sensual love. *Phileo* is brotherly love and kindness. But the word used in this passage is *agape*. That's affection or be-nevolence, a self-sacrificial love. I love the literal Greek transla-tion: "a love feast."

5. a. Look up *feast* in the dictionary. Which part of the defini-tion stands out to you?

Have you ever heard (or said), "I just cannot love that person"? I have. Because we're limited by our own sinful human nature, we can't feel love for everyone. When we turn that around, we must acknowledge that we're not lovable either. But we have the Holy Spirit living inside, and with Him, we have a love feast! (How's *that* for sticking with a food metaphor?)

Satan wants us to believe that we're not lovable, that we're not worthy of the love and forgiveness that our Lord so freely gives us. Satan would rather fill us with the junk food of uncertainty and fear. He would rather distract us with busyness and excuses so we miss the great feast that has been prepared for us. (See Luke 14:15–24.)

While Satan wants us to miss the love feast altogether, Jesus' words on the night before He was betrayed remind us that He poured out His blood for the forgiveness of sins (Matthew 26:27–28). Now that we are freed from our sins, He welcomes us to the feast. But He doesn't simply want to free us from our sin. He also wants to free us from the bondage that comes from holding a sin against a brother or sister, the bondage that comes from being unforgiving.

b. In fact, Jesus says, if you are coming before the altar and remember that your brother has something against you, what should you do first? (See Matthew 5:23–24.)

c. What does this say to you about Christ's invitation to receive Him at His Holy Supper?

d. Now, let's take this a step further. Is there someone you need to invite to the Table right now? Write his or her name here. (Use code if you want to.) You're more accountable, even if only to yourself, if you've committed something to action by writing it down. I'm not saying it will be easy, but don't sell the Holy Spirit short.

The second fruit on the list is **joy**. That word is *chara*, and it's Greek for "cheerfulness, calm delight, great gladness." Our joy doesn't depend on our circumstances. What is the context of joy in each of the following passages?

6. a. John 16:20–22

b. 2 Corinthians 7:4

c. 2 Corinthians 8:2

d. Hebrews 10:34

e. Hebrews 12:2

7. a. Is there a situation you are facing in which you need to find joy outside of your circumstances?

b. Joy is not always found in our circumstances, but it is always found in our Savior. A disgruntled Habakkuk questioned God's goodness (or perceived lack thereof), yet what realization does he reach in Habakkuk 3:17–18?

c. In the same way, where does Isaiah find joy in Isaiah 49:13?

Joy is found in our salvation, and it's found in God's comfort, often expressed through the people He places in our lives, in the midst of our circumstances, people who may have experienced a similar trial (2 Corinthians 1:3–5). Ultimately we can find joy in the "not yet," knowing that one day, there will be no more hunger or thirst, and God will wipe away every tear from our eyes (Revelation 7:15–17).

d. Try praying Romans 15:13. Or pray this verse over someone who is facing such a trial. Write the words here, or paraphrase them in your own words:

Peace comes next. That's *eirene.* It means "peace, quietness, rest; to set at one again." This concept is so important that it appears in every book of the New Testament except 1 John. The apostle Paul used it at the beginning of every one of his letters to the Early Church. Look at the first few verses of Galatians, Ephesians, or Philippians to see how the word is used and in what combination.

8. Write your thoughts here:

"Peace" was a common Hebrew greeting (i.e., *shalom*), but the sentiment is just a word without grace. However, when peace is paired with grace (the freely given, unmerited favor and love of Jesus Christ), it has the power in our lives to overcome the world. Jesus speaks of this peace in His final talk with His disciples before His betrayal.

9. a. What does He say in John 14:27?

b. And what does He say in John 16:33?

The Greek word for **world** is *kosmos,* which means "the orderly arrangement of things." From this root, we get the English words *cosmopolitan* ("sophisticated, urbane, worldly") and *cosmetics* ("powder, lipstick, or other preparations for beautifying; superficial measures that make something appear better, more attractive").

c. The prophets warn about this peace of the world. Jeremiah says, "They have healed the wound of my people lightly, saying, 'Peace, peace,' when there is no peace" (Jeremiah 6:14). That's a cosmetic peace, a cover-up peace. What does Ezekiel say about the peace the world has to offer in Ezekiel 13:10?

When a flimsy wall is built, they cover it with whitewash. That's the world's peace. While it may look good on the outside, there's nothing substantial underneath.

In John 16, then, Jesus says that things that seem sophisticated, worldly, and attractive do not bring lasting peace, and getting caught up in them will bring trouble. On the other hand, He has overcome appearances, and He alone will bring true, lasting peace. In this we can find comfort and confidence. That's what Jesus' words "take heart" say in the Greek.

God's Word tells us about His peace. It comes because the Lord sustains us despite the influence of our enemies (Psalm 3:5–6; 4:8). It comes when our mind is **stayed** ("propped on, leaning on, resting on, taking hold of") on Him (Isaiah 26:3). Peace comes over and over in the New Testament as Jesus says, "Your faith has saved you; go in peace" (Luke 7:50, for example). Most of all, peace comes because Jesus' death on the cross restored the harmony between God and man that was lost when Adam and Eve sinned (Colossians 1:19–20).

10. a. What picture does Isaiah give in 11:6–9 of the true peace that comes through the Prince of Peace?

b. What does this mean to you in the context of your life today?

Remember, Jesus has left you with the gift of His Spirit and peace as an outcome of faith in Him. This week, be sure to pick up some love, joy, and peace "fruit." Remember, there's plenty available! "Taste and see that the LORD is good!" (Psalm 34:8). You will be blessed.

STOCKING UP ON THE FRUIT OF THE SPIRIT,
PART 2

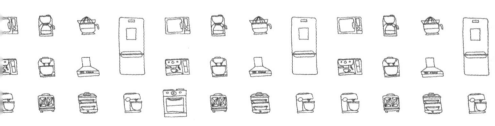

When my son was three, he was a terrible eater. Okay, he's *still* a terrible eater—and he's nine—but one day when he was three, my frustration came to a head. My parents were visiting for Easter, and my mom volunteered to make the meal on Good Friday, a family tradition of egg pancakes. I think my life was lacking several of the spiritual fruits that day. You may be able to pick them out as I tell the rest of my tale. (Write the missing fruit in the parentheses.)

We sat down to dinner, and Matthew wouldn't eat. Not one bite. Irritation built up in me as I felt I was somehow failing as a mom. (_____) Emotions boiled to the surface and I erupted. (_____) Time was short since we had to leave soon for church. (_____) (Sometimes we think a steady diet of church will replace the fruit of the Spirit.) I ranted; I raved; I tried to cajole, shame, and, yes, even *force* Matt to eat. I picked up a bite of food and tried to stuff it into his mouth. (This is becoming too painful for me to continue.) Who was this lunatic that had taken over my body? My mom, dad, and even my husband stared at me. I didn't even recognize myself. It certainly wasn't one of my finer moments as a mom or even as a human being.

I learned two things that day: (a) I need more fruit of the Spirit in my life, and (b) you cannot force someone to eat. If you've tried, then you know it isn't pretty—for either of you. The funny thing is, now Matt *loves* egg pancakes and usually eats more than anyone else.

Like my son, I often choose to reject the abundant goodness

God has placed before me. I close my eyes, cover my mouth (sometimes even sticking out my tongue in defiance), or turn my back to the table. No matter how hungry I may be for God's fruit in my life, on my own, I reject it. That's sin. It disconnects me from God. In fact, "The mind that is set on the flesh is hostile to God, for it does not submit to God's law; indeed, it cannot" (Romans 8:7).

Isaiah lays out the problem in the form of a question, in terms I can easily understand: "Why do you spend your money for that which is not bread, and your labor for that which does not satisfy?" (Isaiah 55:2a). I'm looking for a quick fix for my craving, but what I find doesn't truly satisfy. Isaiah continues, "Listen diligently to me, and eat what is good, and delight yourselves in rich food" (v. 2b). I like the way it's stated in the NIV: "and your soul will delight in the richest of fare." God offers me **soul food**. By the Holy Spirit's power, I am able to come to the table and eat, to "Taste and see that the LORD is good" (Psalm 34:8).

Every time we kneel at the Lord's Table to celebrate Holy Communion, we are reminded of His words: "Take, eat; this is My body. . . . This is My blood . . . poured out for many for the forgiveness of sins" (Matthew 26:26–28). It is by that forgiveness, and filled with the Holy Spirit, that my life can indeed display the fruit of the Spirit.

BiBLe STuDY QueStioNS

Begin by reviewing the fruit of the Spirit. (If you need a reminder, turn to Galatians 5:22–23.)

I like today's first fruit so much better in the ESV and NIV translations than the KJV. While the ESV calls the next fruit "**patience**," the KJV calls it "**longsuffering**." There's nothing about suffering that makes it desirable. Have you noticed that grocers no longer call prunes "prunes"? That word conjures up all sorts of negative images. Grocers now call prunes "dried plums." It's the same fruit—only the name has been changed to protect the squeamish.

The same can be said for longsuffering/patience. I have a confession to make to you. (What's another confession among friends?) When I pray for patience, I don't pray for God to make me long-suffering. I pray for Him to take away whatever is causing my impatience. For example, "God, give me patience with my daughter today when she insists on having her own way" is really my way of saying, "God, please keep Brianna from being stubborn today."

What are you really praying for when you pray for patience? Are you like many people I know who say they don't pray for patience because when they do, God always gives them something to be patient *through*?

My dictionary defines **patience** as "the bearing of provocation, annoyance, misfortune or pain without complaint, loss of temper, irritability or the like."

Today is a perfect day for me to pluck the fruit of patience and enjoy its sweet taste. My daughter (whom I love) woke me at 3:45 a.m. to show me what the tooth fairy brought her last night. After I went back to bed, she woke her brother to tell him (despite my telling her to do otherwise—but I've already mentioned her stubbornness). At around 4:45 a.m., they both came bounding down the stairs, only to be sent back to bed by a less-than-forbearing mother. Despite my efforts, there was no more sleep in our house. My husband awoke barely able to move because of back pain (another long story, so I'll skip those details). And it's raining. Dear Lord, I need a double serving of that fruit—and I need it now!

The Greek word for *patience* implies "with long [enduring] temper." A pastor friend says, "Patience is having a long fuse." Remembering how long God's fuse has been for you may enable you to grab the Holy Spirit's longer fuse as well.

1. What do you learn about God's long fuse in each of the following passages? What incentive does each give you to receive more patience?

a. Romans 9:22–23

b. 1 Timothy 1:16

c. 2 Peter 3:9, 15

2. a. Is there a person or situation calling for you to exercise patience today? (Almost every situation ultimately boils down to a person: a relative, neighbor, co-worker, or a person working for a government agency, etc.) Describe it here:

Now, pause the digital video recorder of your life. (Do you know about this handy device? The DVR allows you to pause live television and replay it later. Cool, huh? Often after experiencing impatience, I wish I had one of these in my life.) Reread the Romans 9 passage carefully, keeping in mind the situation you just wrote about above. Let's suppose that God was in your situation. What if God, wanting to show His **wrath** *(orge,* "passion, indignation, righteous anger") toward this person/situation and make His power known, instead bore the provocation without complaint or loss of temper toward the object of His wrath?

And what if He did it to make known the **riches** *(ploutos,* "abundance, wealth, fullness")* of His mercy and compassion toward this person? And what if this was His plan all along, to bring glory to His name? And what if the purpose of His kindness was to lead to repentance (Romans 2:4)? And what if you admit that on at least one occasion, God has shown that exact same patience toward you?

b. Now, "unpause the DVR," and put yourself back in the situation. Knowing that your patience might lead to God's glory, how will you respond to this person today?

c. Finally, as you face people or situations that make you impatient, try saying Ephesians 4:2. You may need to keep repeating it to lengthen your fuse. Write the words here. Writing it out is the first step to memorizing it.

3. a. After patience, the Holy Spirit gives us **kindness**. Write your own brief description of kindness:

If your description is like mine, it describes someone who is good, considerate, and loving. The kind person speaks in a loving way to everyone and is always ready with a helping hand. She brings the casserole to the family in crisis, holds the crying baby for its mother, and offers to go to the grocery store to pick up a few things for you.

The Greek word is *chrestotes* and primarily means "usefulness," then "moral excellence in character and demeanor." That definition seems to set the bar very high. Lest you think that some people are just born kind but you do not have that particular spiritual gift, consider Romans 3:10–12. The word translated "good" here is the same one used for *kindness* in Galatians 5:22.

b. What does it say about our ability to be kind?

c. Titus 3:4–5 also speaks of God's kindness to us. Why does God's kindness and love appear?

d. In truth, it is *only* through the power of the Holy Spirit in our lives that we can display this fruit. As God's chosen people, what can we do? (See Colossians 3:12–13.)

We display the fruit of kindness when we act in a kind way, when we show compassion and tenderness, offer sympathy, are generous, and do a good turn, all by the power of the Holy Spirit. Notice that kindness is not a *feeling* but a *behavior*. Action accompanies kindness.

Goodness comes next. This Greek word emphasizes an intrinsic virtue, coming from one's very nature. Where *kindness* is a chosen action, *goodness* is an internal value that can show itself in our actions. Luke 6:43–45 explains.

4. a. What example does Jesus use for goodness?

b. In Acts 11:22–24, how do we see goodness play out in the life of Barnabas?

c. According to Hebrews 13:20–21, where does that goodness come from?

In fact, the word translated "**equip**" in v. 21 is *katartizo*. It means "to complete thoroughly, repair, or adjust." When I pray for God to help me pick this fruit of the Spirit, I'm asking Him for an internal attitude adjustment. Goodness isn't a trait I'm born with; it's a trait I'm reborn with.

d. Name an area in your life that could use a new attitude right now. Then pray for the Holy Spirit to make the adjustment. You can write your own simple prayer here:

Know that God is able to make that adjustment. He is able to do immeasurably more than all we can ask or imagine (Ephesians 3:20), to supply every need according to His glorious riches in Jesus Christ (Philippians 4:19).

5. a. God attaches a reward to the next fruit. Look at Revelation 2:10 and write the second half of the verse here:

Faithfulness: the Greek word is *pistis*, and it means "persuasion, moral conviction, especially reliance upon Christ for salvation and constancy in such profession."

b. Hebrews 11:1 gives another definition. What is it?

Where does faith come from, according to the following verses?

c. Ephesians 2:8–9

d. Hebrews 12:2

Jesus is indeed the author and perfecter of our faith. The first several verses of Hebrews 12 are almost a pep talk in the middle of this event we call life, with all its trials and sorrows. "Don't give up. Don't give in. Keep your eyes on Jesus, the prize, and don't lose heart."

6. a. The most difficult thing about this fruit is that we often don't know we have it until it is tested. Read 1 Peter 1:6–7; what is this fruit all about?

b. The NIV says, "so that your faith . . . may be **proved** genuine." Here's a question for your consideration: who are you proving it to? Among the definitions of *prove* in my dictionary are "to establish the genuineness of; to give demonstration by action; to show (oneself) to have a characteristic of, especially through one's actions."

c. What does this fruit enable us to do? (See Ephesians 6:16.)

Life this side of heaven is difficult. Jesus Himself warns us about this in John 16:33: "In the world you will have tribulation." The first half of Revelation 2:10 is, in effect, a warning that "it's going to get tough. You're going to suffer. The devil will throw everything he has at you. Don't be afraid. Be faithful. Be faithful!" Since faith is proved genuine through trials, one of the most loving gifts we can give someone who is facing such trials, whose world is being rocked by adversity, is to pray for her to stand firm in her faith. While going through the trial, she may not have the strength to pray this for herself.

Oh, what we've done to the English language! Words that were meant as positive now have ugly undertones. Words that were compliments become derogatory. I'm sure you can name a few words that, once benign, can no longer be uttered in polite society.

While translated "**gentleness**" in the ESV, my *Strong's Concordance* tells me the original Greek word used here means "humble, meek." (It's translated "meekness" in the KJV.) But my Random House dictionary says **meek** is "overly submissive or compliant; spiritless; tame." I don't believe these are qualities one usually aspires to in our current culture. **Humble** doesn't fair much better, with synonyms such as "submissive, unassuming, plain, common, poor" and a definition that states, "having a feeling of insignificance, inferiority, subservience, etc."

One of the reasons these words have taken on such less-than-desirable meanings is that the current world sees them as unflattering characteristics. In a world of celebrity and power struggle, we are taught to toot our own horn because no one else will. We idolize the rich and famous and worship those who are winners and champions. The titles of our television shows reflect this cultural shift. *Star Search* has been replaced by *American Idol*. Whereas a star shines brightly, an idol is worshiped—and anything less is not good enough. Yet, our Lord, who left heaven to take on human weakness and humiliation for our sake, tells us the fruit of the Spirit is humility.

7. What does God's Word tell us about this characteristic in each of the following verses?

a. Psalm 25:9

b. Psalm 37:11 (which Jesus quotes in Matthew 5:5)

c. Matthew 11:29

8. a. The last few words in the passage from Matthew show a side benefit of humility: "you will find rest for your souls." How does rest spring out of gentleness and humility?

b. Based on 1 Peter 3:3–4, how might you find more rest for your soul?

c. Is there an area where you need the Holy Spirit to help you stop striving, to clothe yourself in humility? (See Colossians 3:12.)

d. Although 1 Peter 5:5–7 originally was written to those who are "younger" (and you may not think this applies to you), what does God say He'll do? If this makes you anxious, be sure you take to heart the promise of verse 7.

Finally, Paul speaks of **self-control**. I think the biggest problem with self-control is that word *self*. Many of my problems in this area come from thinking I am able, by myself, to control myself; that I am able to exercise restraint, dominate, command, hold in check, curb. It's all about me. I am in the world, but I have forgotten the words of 1 John 5:19, "the whole world is under the control of the evil one" (NIV).

By myself, I am unable to exercise restraint over things like my eating habits, gossip, my temper, how much I watch TV, where my thoughts wander, and how much money I spend. Proverbs 25:28 describes what I am like: "Like a city whose walls are broken down is a man [or woman] who lacks self-control" (NIV). There are cracks all over my walls. I let the devil trick me into thinking that applying some paint of restraint, order, or control will cover them, but without proper mending, the cracks just show again.

9. a. What about you? In what area do you find yourself unable to control yourself?

Now, with your permission, I'd like to expand this thought a bit. Let's start by replacing "self-control" with the concept of "God-control." When I pluck this spiritual fruit, I'm turning my focus on myself over to God, submitting to His will, and asking Him to transform me through the work of the Holy Spirit. He is able where I am not.

b. What does Philippians 3:20–21 say?

Certainly a God who can make the winds and the waves obey Him (Matthew 8:27) can transform me as I believe and put my trust in Him.

10. This leads me directly back to Galatians 5:25. If I live by the Spirit, what should I do?

If I'm not trying to control where I go, I'm free to follow in the Spirit's steps. I like the imagery here. The Greek word is *stoicheo*, and it means "to march in (military) rank, to conform to, to walk orderly." My life certainly needs a little more order, and God has, from the beginning, made order from chaos. God who created the world will re-create my life as well.

You know those first words of the Bible: "In the beginning, God created the heavens and the earth. The earth was without form and void" (Genesis 1:1–2). **"Void"** is *bohuw*, which means "to be empty, a vacuum, an indistinguishable ruin." What I can take away from that verse is that God doesn't need a "good me" to start with. He doesn't need me to get myself halfway there so He can finish the job. Absolutely not! He created the world with a word, and He will take this indistinguishable ruin and re-create me with a word as well—the Word made flesh, Jesus Christ (John 1:14).

TAKE ME AWAY
GETTING A FRESH WIND OF THE SPIRIT

"Calgon, take me away!" I shout—if not aloud, then at least in my mind's ear—recalling a successful advertising campaign from my youth. The picture is of a woman resting happily in a deep bubble bath despite the cacophony just outside the bathroom door.

Sometimes I need a Calgon break, perhaps from the same cacophony. The kids are fighting with each other, or I with them. The housework is waiting. I have chauffeuring to do . . . or shopping . . . or bills to pay . . . or all of the above. People want pieces of my time; stresses and worries war with my soul. These are the moments when I feel as if I've lost a piece of my mind, and I've definitely lost my *peace* of mind. Fill in your own blank—from what do you need to escape right now?

I'm the queen of vacations. Take 'em early and often, that's my motto! National parks, the beach, a visit with family and friends—*where* is irrelevant; just getting away is what's important. Sometimes I even need a vacation from my vacation! This summer was an example: 5,400 miles in the car . . . 109 hours driving . . . 2 countries . . . 11 states . . . white water rafting . . . jet skiing . . . boating . . . camping . . . walking around the national mall in Washington DC . . . touring a science museum . . . visiting an amusement park . . . attending a family reunion . . . enjoying a reunion with college friends . . . whew! I'm worn out just writing about it!

And who among us hasn't taken a vacation with great anticipation and returned with unmet expectations? One summer, while taking a trip to Canada, we made a side trip to Glacier National

Park (which I call one of the most beautiful places on earth). My husband hadn't been there before, and as we drove through the park to get to our lodging, it was getting dark. "Don't worry," I told him, "we can see the mountains tomorrow." So we didn't stop at any of the pull-offs to drink in the scenery. The next morning, we awoke to a thick covering of clouds. As we drove up into the mountains, we couldn't even see them! And when we arrived at the visitor's center at the top of the pass, it was snowing—despite the fact that it was late June. Mark never did see the mountains. Not even a glimpse. And we never saw the Na Pali Coast on Kauai, Hawaii, either, as there were thick clouds and rain there, despite everyone telling us, "It never rains on the *whole* island." Flight delays, altitude sickness, inclement weather, bickering children, car trouble, traffic snarls—all these can lead to unmet expectations and less-than-restful vacations.

Does it seem to you that there are times you can get away but still not find rest? That's when what is needed is not a break from the routine, but a breath of fresh air. At these times, it's not mountain air we need to breathe, but a fresh wind of the Spirit, a breath from God.

BiBLe STuDY QuesTioNS

1. a. Before we go further, let's establish a word. In Genesis 1:2, what was "hovering over the face of the waters"?

In Hebrew, the word used for *spirit* is *ruwach*. Exodus 15:8 describes the parting of the Red Sea: "At the **blast** of Your nostrils the waters piled up." It's the same word. Again, in verse 10, "You blew with Your **wind**," it's the same word. In fact, that word appears 348 times in the Old Testament. It is generally translated as either "spirit" (not always with a capital *s*), "wind," or "breath." Keep this in mind as we continue.

b. Right from the start, from "In the beginning," what is it that gives us life? (See Genesis 2:7.)

Here the word is different. It's *naphach*, and it means "to puff." Later in the sentence, it's *neshamah*, "a puff." God puffed a puff of air into us—He breathed life into us. He resuscitated us. We were lifeless until He breathed life into us. Job 33:4 says, "The Spirit [*ruwach*] of God has made me, and the breath [*neshamah*] of the Almighty gives me life." We are not alive without God's breath.

However, we can be alive (physically breathing) without being filled with the breath of God. The prophet Elijah once found himself greatly in need of the breath of the Spirit.

Elijah, whose very name meant "the Lord is my God," knew what it was to be close to God. As God's representative, he had said, "As the LORD, the God of Israel, lives, before whom I stand, there shall be neither dew nor rain in these years, except by my word" (1 Kings 17:1). And it was so. As the land was starved for water, Elijah withdrew from the people to a ravine, where ravens brought him bread and meat and he was able to drink water from the brook.

During this time of drought in Israel, Elijah didn't experience drought himself. Instead, he saw God's provision for a widow with a jar of oil that never ran out, and he raised her son from the dead. Then, in the third year of the drought, he did the most spectacular thing: single-handedly (okay, it was *God's* single hand!), Elijah took on 450 priests of Baal. Elijah was able to display the powerlessness of Baal and the awesomeness of God in a giant barbecue. (You can read the whole story in 1 Kings 18:16–39.)

When God proved to the priests that He was indeed the powerful God Elijah had declared Him to be, all the people cried out, "The LORD, He is God" (v. 39), and God, through Elijah, once again sent rain to the land.

2. Our need for "fresh air" could come after an incredibly joyful season. Remember that Elijah had just shown everyone how powerful God is. Have you experienced a joyful, exciting event and then, right after it, had a "Calgon moment"—a need to withdraw from the scene for just a little while? (A wedding, a women's retreat, and the birth of a child are all joyful, big events, but any one of them could deplete your energy and leave you lifeless.) Describe it here:

Now, let's get the whole story from this point on. Read 1 Kings 19:1–18.

3. a. Elijah's need for "a breath of fresh air" doesn't begin because of a joyous event, although he had just had "a mountain-top experience." What message does Jezebel send him? (See vv. 1–2.)

b. What is Elijah's reaction? (See v. 3.)

"He was afraid . . . and **ran** for his life" (v. 3). *Yalak* has many definitions, among which is "vanish." I can easily imagine why Elijah would just want to vanish in this moment.

c. A similar expression is used in Genesis 19:17. What event is happening here?

d. The sense of urgency is again apparent. Although I've often heard the expression in movies, I've never had the experience in real life, but I imagine some of you may have felt the need to "run for your life." If so, what was the event, and what were the emotions involved?

4. a. After fleeing for a day, Elijah is at the end of his rope. What are his words? (See 1 Kings 19:4.)

The KJV expresses it in very matter-of-fact fashion: "he requested for himself that he might die." I cannot imagine it being uttered in such an emotionless tone.

b. Moses utters the same sentiment. What are his words in Numbers 11:10–15?

Now *that's* a bit more my style—a little ranting and raving at God. No matter if calm or ranting, I can so relate to Moses and Elijah. It seems to be my life as a mom. "O God," I cry, "my work is fruitless. No one listens to me. Why should I bother anymore? I've had enough!"

c. When have you said the same? (You're having a Calgon moment!)

5. a. One solution to end the stress is to sleep. Jacob did (Genesis 28:11). He was so tired that he used a stone as a pillow and slept. Elijah slept as well (1 Kings 19:5). Even Jesus needed to sleep (Matthew 8:24). What does God tell us in Psalm 127:2?

I picture myself as a crying baby, fighting to stay awake, yet too tired to sleep. God gently picks me up, rocks me, rubs my back, and sometimes even holds me tightly to Himself to still me so I can sleep.

b. Where does your stress come from? Are you a new mom, mother of a teenager, sandwich generation? Are you wearing the chauffeur's cap, hustling from one activity to another, or are you wearing a judge's robe as you settle disputes? Maybe you're a quarterback at work, calling the plays and hoping you don't get sacked. What's on your list? Could somehow finding a little peace and quiet add wind to your sails?

6. Elijah is awakened by an angel's touch. What does he find? (See 1 Kings 19:6.)

The word used here for **angel** is *malak*; it means "to dispatch as a deputy, a messenger, specifically of God." Maybe you could use an angel to bring you a meal. Or perhaps you know someone for whom you could be God's messenger, bringing God's love in the form of a meal. I have a friend who was feeling a bit down and forgotten. As a parent of several very small children, her life was full. It happened to be her birthday, and while she knew her husband would do something for her later, during the middle of the day, she was feeling alone despite the presence of her children who were too young to even wish her a happy birthday. At that moment, a neighbor who worked at a bakery stopped by with a beautiful "surplus" cake (ordered but cancelled), not even knowing that it was her birthday, but just thinking she might enjoy a sweet treat. At that moment, my friend felt so incredibly loved by God that He would see her in her distress and gift her with such a simple thing. Can you do something simple and similar for someone? If so, write her name here. Then, don't just think about it—do it!

7. a. After eating and drinking and more rest, Elijah is once again strengthened, ready for a forty-day journey. Notice that food and rest have restored his physical strength, but Elijah is still in need of that "breath of air," that wind of the Spirit. His journey takes him to Horeb, the mountain of God. What does he do that night? (See v. 9.)

b. Who else found himself at Mount Horeb? Read Exodus 3:1–6 to refresh your memory as to what happened there.

c. The same cave may very well play a role in another Bible story. If you have maps in your Bible, find Mount Horeb and Mount Sinai. (They are on the Sinai Peninsula.) Then read Exodus 33:18–23; what happens there?

8. a. Back to Elijah. He has rested, and he's been strengthened by food, but he's still not really refreshed. His spirit is still in despair. What does God say to Elijah? (See 1 Kings 19:9.)

b. What is Elijah's response? Without using his exact words, how would you describe what Elijah is feeling?

Maybe you are serving God in your family, the Church, a small group, as a Sunday School teacher, or as a leader in some other capacity. You've done everything you thought you were sup-posed to do, but it seems like it's all to no avail. As coordinator of the Sunday School, you recruit teachers, assemble materials, plan programs, but all you hear are complaints about what's gone wrong. As president of the PTA, the bickering over dif-ferences of opinion on how something must be done is stealing your joy; a lack of volunteers is making you despair; and low turnout at programs is making you wonder if it's all worth it. From where you're standing right now, it seems as if God is not blessing your service. Sound familiar?

c. What is God's response? (See v. 11.)

What He told Elijah, He also told Moses in Exodus 33:19. (Take a minute to check it out for yourself.) Maybe Elijah expected God to pick him up and place him in the cleft of the rock, as He had Moses. Surely he expected to see Him in a big way—af-ter all, this is the God who sustained him for three years; who worked through him to raise a boy from the dead; who had just proved His power before hundreds of Baal-worshiping Israelites. So Elijah looks. And waits.

9. a. What comes first—and what does it do? (See 1 Kings 19:11.)

That wind is *ruwach*, our word that is sometimes translated as "spirit"—but the Spirit of God is not there. Sometimes God is in the wind, and sometimes the winds just break our **rocks** into pieces. The word here is *cela*. It could mean "fortress" or "stronghold."

b. Are you currently experiencing a great wind? Is it breaking down your fortress? your stronghold? Write about it here:

After the wind comes an **earthquake**—that's *raash*, "a vibration, bounding, uproar; a commotion, a confused noise." Sometimes God comes in the midst of the confusion, but sometimes what's going on is just a lot of commotion.

After the earthquake comes a fire. But God does not show Himself there either. Do you think Elijah may have been disappointed again? He expected to see God in the wind, in the earthquake, in the fire. He expected God to use one of those means to wipe out his enemies. Sometimes our disappointment with God is just about unmet expectations. It's not that God's not acting on our behalf, it's just that He's not acting in the way we expect He should. I confess, I have hoped for God to cause defeat or pain to my children to teach them a lesson, and I've been (mildly) disappointed when He chose not to act that way.

c. Do you recall a time when you were disappointed that God didn't act in a big way to smite your enemies? Describe that time here:

Perhaps Elijah has become addicted to the *"wow!"* so he's looking for God in all the wrong places. Yet, after the fire comes a **"gentle whisper"** (v. 12, NIV), a **"still small voice"** (KJV). The word translated "voice" or "whisper" is *qol*. It can mean a variety of sounds—from a "bleating" or a "lowing" (remember the cattle in "Away in a Manger"?), to "thunder" (that's how it is used in Exodus 9:23); from "a proclamation" to "a song."

d. What is Elijah's reaction to the gentle whisper? (See 1 Kings 19:13.)

e. What was Moses' reaction when he heard from God in Exodus 3:6?

A "Calgon moment" is a moment when you are ready to hear from God, to be filled with the fresh wind of His Spirit. Once again, a voice *(qol)* asks, "What are you doing here, Elijah?" Elijah's response is the same. But this time, his humbled heart is ready to hear God speak.

f. How does God answer each of Elijah's complaints? (See 1 Kings 19:15–18.)

God says, "First, We're going to anoint a new king; then We're going to get some help, someone who will succeed you so that your work will go on after you are gone." And, finally, He says, "You are not the only one left. Seven thousand others have not worshiped Baal."

The disciples, too, needed a fresh wind of the Spirit. Jesus had died, risen from the dead, and ascended into heaven. Certainly their joy at seeing Jesus again after His resurrection and the wonder of watching Him being taken up into heaven before their very eyes (Acts 1:9) left them with a sense of "What next?" They were left wondering what Jesus had meant when He said, "You will receive power when the Holy Spirit has come upon you, and you will be My witnesses" (v. 8).

The New Testament word translated **Spirit**, *pneuma*, you guessed it, can also be translated "breath" or "breeze." And so they waited for God to breathe on them again, to restore their lives. And He does. Read the account of the beginning of this event called Pentecost in Acts 2:1–4.

10. a. In verse 2, what do they hear?

b. The **wind** is *pnoe*, also translated "breath," and it has the same Greek root as *pneuma*. As God breathed into the room, the sound filled the entire house. With what were the disciples filled, and what were they able to do?

Speaking in languages they'd never known before (v. 6); proclaiming Christ boldly, while weeks before, they had denied even knowing Him (Matthew 26:69–74); repenting and receiving forgiveness (Acts 2:38–40)—all these come with a fresh wind of the Spirit.

c. What was the outcome of that day, and how did they continue in the Spirit? (See vv. 41–47.)

John 3:8 tells us, "The wind blows where it wishes. . . . So it is with everyone who is born of the Spirit." The Holy Spirit is sovereign. We cannot tell Him when to appear or where to go. He works as He pleases in the human heart.

But we can seek God's face—in prayer. Jesus knew that; over and over, we are told, "He went by Himself to pray." We can also seek God in His Word. Jeremiah 15:16 says, "Your words were found, and I ate them, and Your words became to me a joy and the delight of my heart." Do you feast on God's Word, or are you having just an occasional snack?

We seek God's face when we approach the Lord's Table in Holy Communion and let Him refresh and restore us there with His forgiveness and grace. We can be filled with the fresh breath of the Spirit as we sing psalms, hymns, and spiritual songs and make melody to the Lord with our hearts (Ephesians 5:18–19).

God wants us to place our hope in Him. David tells us, "On God rests my salvation and my glory; my mighty rock, my refuge is God. Trust in Him at all times, O people; pour out your heart before Him; God is a refuge for us" (Psalm 62:7–8). In both verses, **"refuge"** is *machceh*. It means "a shelter, a hope." My English dictionary gives as synonyms for *refuge* these words: "retreat, sanctuary, haven." What a great place to take a vacation! And it's a getaway you can get away to without leaving your house.

d. What about you? How has God answered you in a "Calgon moment" and given you the breath of air that you are seeking? Has He come in a calm silence or a thunder? a proclamation? a song? Write about it here:

Remember my husband's experience in Glacier National Park? Although he never saw the top of the mountains, he still got a glimpse of heaven that day. He chose to see the little things: the deer in the bushes, the tiny speck of a grizzly bear way off in the valley, the beautiful flowers springing up in the cracks of the rocks, the tiny waterfall. And his words at the end of the day were "It's a bit like heaven. Here on earth, we only can catch a glimpse, but one day we will see it in full." I think he had a Calgon moment!

AFTERWORD

Friends, I pray that if you did this study with a small group, you found yourselves laughing together. Maybe you even shed a few tears together. I hope that you will continue to meet together, perhaps around another Bible study, or simply gathering around the Word of God at church, in someone's living room, or maybe at a local coffee shop. The place you meet is less important than whom you meet—the living God, who promises, "Draw near to God, and He will draw near to you" (James 4:8). Most of all, I hope you will continue to open the eyes of your heart to God's working in your lives, wherever you are and whatever you are doing.

"I pray also that the eyes of your heart may be enlightened in order that you may know the hope to which He has called you, the riches of His glorious inheritance in the saints, and His incomparably great power for us who believe" (Ephesians 1:18–19a NIV).

May God bless all of your days!
Susan

LEADER'S NOTES

Session 1: The Color Purple, Part 1

1. We cannot hope to get our spiritual laundry clean unless we first admit we need to throw something in the wash. We must confess our sins.

2. a. None of us is righteous. No one does good. Jesus reminds us of this in Mark 10:18, saying, "No one is good except God alone." The list continues with Scriptures cited from the Old Testament. Everyone is guilty before God.

b. "This people draw near with their mouth and honor Me with their lips, while their hearts are far from Me.

c. Answers will vary.

3. a–c. Answers will vary.

4. a. Unconfessed sin will eventually erode and decay our physical and emotional health. Confession, though, results in forgiveness.

b. Similarly, we often deny that something is a sin (we may call it "a mistake," "an error in judgment," "a choice," etc.); we may say "it's only a little thing," or "not as bad as someone else"; we may spread gossip and call it "a prayer request"; we may even say, "But I was only trying to help." All of these deceptions keep us from confession and repentance—and thus from the mercy of forgiveness.

5. On our own, we're sunk! Jesus asks why their faith is so weak.

6. a. Break down the altars, burn the idols. Completely destroy them.

b. Don't turn after these useless things; they cannot rescue you.

7. Even while they are worshiping the Lord, they are serving idols, and their children do likewise. How often parents pass on the "worry gene" to their children, and a new generation of idol worshipers is created!

8. We exchange our glory for worthless idols. When worry becomes our god, we exchange our glory for worry, forgetting our Savior and the

great things He has done.

9. a. Worry causes us to forsake the hope available in God's love.

b. "Who of you by worrying can add a single hour to his life?" (NIV).

10. a. and b. We should cast our cares on the Lord.

c. In everything, by prayer and petition, and with thanksgiving, we should present our requests to God. When we can turn our mind to thankfulness for what God has given us, sometimes our worries will melt away.

11. We are washed, sanctified, and justified in Jesus' name.

Session 2: The Color Purple, Part 2

1. We waste away physically.

2. This is desert imagery, a wilderness, oppressive heat and heaviness.

3. a. God asks if these bones can live, and Ezekiel responds that only God knows.

b. God gives Ezekiel the words to speak over the bones to make them live again.

c. Ezekiel followed God's directions and prophesied to the bones. Flesh covered the bones, but there was no breath in them until the Lord breathed on them and they lived.

4. Answers will vary.

5. Answers will vary. Here are mine:

a. realized

b. was intimate with

c. recognize

d. know for certain, have no doubts

e. learn

f. concern yourself with

6. a. It was used to mark the homes for the angel of death to pass over.

b. It was used during the process by which a person was declared cleansed of infectious disease.

c. It was used during the ritual cleansing of an unclean house.

d. It was used during the cleansing ritual for someone who had touched an unclean (dead) body.

e. Moses used it to sprinkle the scroll and the people with blood when he had proclaimed "every commandment of the law" to all the people (v. 19). "Under the law almost everything is purified with blood, and without the shedding of blood there is no forgiveness of sins" (v. 22).

7. Our sins may be blood red, but the Lord will wash us as clean as snow.

8. Jesus cleanses us of our sin; only Jesus can make us clean.

9. a. In Baptism, we are buried with Christ in His death and raised with Him into a new life. In Baptism we are not just cleansed on the outside, but we are changed through and through.

b. "If anyone is in Christ, he is a new creation. The old has passed away; behold, the new has come." (2 Corinthians 5:17)

10. The people who came "out of the great tribulation" were wearing robes that were "made . . . white in the blood of the Lamb."

11. Isaiah also says that he will rejoice in the Lord because He has "clothed me with the garments of salvation; He has covered me with the robe of righteousness." Isaiah uses bride and bridegroom imagery.

Session 3: Getting Rid of Spiritual Bugs

1. a. "Who am I to do this? What if they ask who You are? What if they don't believe me or won't listen to me?" And my personal favorite, "I'm not a good speaker."

To each of these God gives His answer:

b. "I will be with you. It doesn't matter who you are; it's who *I* am."

c. "Tell them 'I AM' has sent you."

d. "If they don't believe you, show them the power of miracles to prove your word."

2. a. Answers will vary.

b. Two are better than one. When one tires or falls, the other can provide companionship, support, encouragement, and even admonishment when warranted. Jesus and leaders of the Early Church also sent workers out two by two.

c. Answers will vary.

d. Jesus says He is with us always, so we are never alone.

3. a. "I don't know how to speak; I'm only a child."

b. "Don't say you are too young. If I send you, you must go. Period. End of discussion."

c. "Don't let anyone look down on you because you are young" (v. 12, NIV).

4. "I have put My words in your mouth."

5. a. He was "beating out wheat in the winepress to hide it from the Midianites."

b. "How can I? My family is the weakest, and I'm the runt of the litter!" (Have *you* ever told God He had the wrong gal?)

c. Saul is "hidden . . . among the baggage."

d. Answers will vary.

6. a. "mighty man of valor" (ESV) or "mighty warrior" (NIV)

b. Answers will vary.

c. The NIV says, "Go in the strength you have" (Judges 6:14). God's big strength + Gideon's puny strength = enough strength. When a parent asks a small child to help carry something, it's rarely because the parent needs the child's strength.

d. Too afraid to act in broad daylight, he waits until it is dark.

e. So that Israel may not boast about her own strength having saved her. Paul says the same in 2 Corinthians 12:7–10.

f. Answers will vary.

7. They were upset and frightened.

8. a. David keeps his eyes on God, not the man (albeit giant) in front of him. "Who is *this* guy to defy God?"

b. He remembered how God had delivered him in the past.

c. In effect, David tells Goliath, "You may come at me with sword, a spear, and a javelin, but my weapon is stronger: I come in the name of the Lord Almighty, the God of the armies of Israel."

d. He runs toward the battle line, and then he fells Goliath with his shepherd's sling and stones.

e. Each verse begins by telling us that "David inquired of the Lord."

9. Answers will vary. Among them: I am not alone. God is with me and He is sending me. It's His strength, not my strength; His words, not my words. I have a history with God, so I can remember how He has been with me in the past. Keep my eyes on God, not on the thing I fear.

Session 4: Cleaning Out the Closet

1. a. The children of Israel weren't rejecting Samuel, they were rejecting God.

b. They wanted to be like other nations.

c. He's a Benjamite. His father is a man of standing named Kish. Saul was an impressive young man, without equal in Israel, a head taller than the others. (He was physically of kingly stature.)

d. Answers will vary. Saul searches high and low for the missing donkeys. This shows persistence and determination. Saul was willing to follow orders, in itself a mark of leadership. When it appears that the donkeys can't be found, he suggests that they return home so his absence doesn't cause his father to worry unnecessarily.

2. a. He asks why he would be addressed in such a way.

b. Answers will vary.

3. a. Saul is seated at the head of the table, and the cook is told to get the special piece of meat he'd prepared. Samuel knew in advance that "the one" would come today.

b. The thigh is part of the fellowship offering and is to be offered to the priest.

c. He would meet two men who will tell him where the donkeys are. Then he would meet three men "going up to God." Finally, he would meet some prophets, and he would wind up prophesying with them.

d. They will be given the Holy Spirit and will be Jesus' witnesses.

4. a. He did join the prophets and prophesy. Everyone who formerly knew him said, "Who is this guy?"

b. He still made excuses (v. 14); he didn't tell his uncle he'd been anointed king (v. 16); he hid among the baggage (v. 22); when trouble-makers threatened, Saul kept silent (v. 27). Maybe he still didn't think he had a right to be king, or that he was good enough, and so on.

5. a. To the Lord God, of course!

b. Samuel reminds the people to fear the Lord and to be faithful servants to Him. He reminds them of God's provision and His power.

6. a. Israel "had become a stench to the Philistines."

b. The last time he attacked strongly, he was praised as a great victor.

c. They hide, flee, and tremble.

d. Answers will vary.

e. David keeps his eyes on God. "Salvation belongs to the LORD" (Psalm 3:8).

7. a. Samuel had told him that he must wait seven days at Gilgal, then Samuel would come.

b. Answers will vary.

c. Don't be afraid; you are worth far more than a sparrow, yet not one of them falls to the ground that the Father doesn't know about.

d. Answers will vary.

e. Answers will vary and may include: he offers up burnt offerings, which only the priest was to do; he starts making excuses, blaming Samuel's tardiness; he says he "forgot" to ask for God's favor, and so forth.

f. Answers will vary.

8. a. "Fear the LORD and serve Him faithfully."

b. Because Saul was foolish and did not keep God's command, God rejected him.

9. a. We are "a new creation" in Christ.

b. Answers will vary.

c. "Put to death . . . what is earthly in you." Don't even leave that stuff in your closet; take it out and bury it!

10. a. The blood of Christ—His death is the cost.

b. In Baptism, we have put on Christ.

c. Answers will vary.

d. Love!

Session 5: Mrs. Fix-it

1. a. Answers will vary.

b. Besides those listed with the question, answers could include "stepping across a boundary, alienation, spit, rift, schism, or dissension." All of these are synonyms for *breach*.

2. a. He found no man.

b. God says, "I will pour out My wrath . . . and consume them with My fiery anger" (Ezekiel 22:31 NIV). God will turn their sin against them.

c. They had forgotten the God who saved them, who had done great things for them in Egypt.

d. God would have destroyed them.

e. Moses stood in the breach before Him.

f. Answers will vary.

3. a. The exiles are in trouble. The walls have been broken down, the gate destroyed by fire.

b. Nehemiah weeps, mourns, fasts, and then prays.

c. Nehemiah confesses the sins of Israel, and "Even I and my father's house have sinned" (v. 6). He says they have acted wickedly, and they have not obeyed God's commands and decrees.

d. Answers will vary.

4. a. He had a sadness of heart. He held his mission in awe and fear, coming before the king in a humble way, with a sad face.

b. He prayed before he spoke.

c. They are quite unhappy.

5. a. He didn't tell anyone what God had put on his heart to do. He didn't say anything about it to anyone.

b. and c. Answers will vary. Talking to friends may bring on fear; "We seem like grasshoppers to them" (see Numbers 13:33). We may blow a situation out of proportion or even downplay the significance of a situation.

d. "God had put into my heart."

e. "Unless the LORD builds the house, those who build it labor in vain."

6. a. They try and turn the problem into a rebellion, twisting the situation for their own gain.

b. When Jesus said that Jairus's daughter was not dead but sleeping, they laughed at Him and scorned Him, mocked and ridiculed Him.

c. He turns the situation over to God, giving God credit, and telling Sanballat and his friends that they have no claim in Jerusalem; in other words, "Move along. God is here, and I don't need your dissension."

7. a. He prays and sets a guard.

b. Their strength is failing.

c. He stations some at the lowest point of the wall and at the exposed places, posting them with their families so that they wouldn't go it alone, and arms them with swords, spears, and bows.

8. Answers will vary. Notice that in *our* spiritual battles, we have the same "armor" from God.

9. a. Answers will vary.

b. Each says, in essence, "Don't be afraid. The Lord your God fights for you." The words of 2 Chronicles 20:15 tell us the battle is not ours, but God's.

10. Answers will vary.

Session 6: Stocking Up on the Fruit of the Spirit, Part 1

1. a. "The fruit of the Spirit is love, joy, peace, patience, kindness, goodness, faithfulness, gentleness, self-control."

b. "What I'm telling you is not too hard or out of reach. When you place My Word in your heart and in your mouth, they will come out of you."

2. a. When I heard the words of the Gospel and believed the message of salvation, I was included in Christ. Once I'm included in Christ, I am given a seal of ownership, that is, the Holy Spirit.

b. The answer is clear: repent, be baptized. Then we know that the Holy Spirit lives in us.

3. a. "I am of the flesh."

b. Answers will vary. Human nature is what we travel in—and what we get caught up in. It's a tangled mess that keeps our lives from flowing smoothly. It keeps my horn honking and my temper flaring. I travel in my humanness rather than riding in my "God-mobile."

c. "I don't do the good I want to do, but I keep on doing the evil I don't want to do. I'm a mess. That's sin living in me."

d. Because of His great love for us, in His grace, and even while we were dead in sin, He has made us alive in Christ.

e. "I'm a wretched person, in need of rescue. Thanks be to God for Jesus Christ!"

4. "You did not choose Me, but I chose you and appointed you that you should go and bear fruit and that your fruit should abide, so that whatever you ask the Father in My name, He may give it to you." (John 15:16)

5. a. The richness and abundance; it is sumptuous and highly agreeable. There's plenty for everyone. It brings delight.

b. Make peace with the one who has sinned against you. Don't come before the altar of the Lord if there is ill will between you and another.

c. and d. Answers will vary.

6. a. We rejoice at new life; no one can take the joy we have at salvation.

b. Despite the problems, Paul experiences joy in the Gospel.

c. Those who have joy in the Lord can't help but help others.

d. Because they had the promise of eternal life in heaven, the destruction of their earthly possessions didn't defeat them.

e. Because He knew the end result—victory over sin, death, and the devil—Jesus could face the agony of death on the cross with joy.

7. a. Answers will vary.

b. Although everything is not "going my way" on the outside, though I don't seem to be prospering, yet I will rejoice in the Lord, the God of my salvation. Not that sometimes joy is a choice of the will—a decision to make—despite the things that are happening around me.

c. Isaiah finds joy in the comfort of the Lord and in God's compassion.

d. "May the God of hope fill you with all joy and peace in believing, so that by the power of the Holy Spirit you may abound in hope." (Romans 15:13)

8. Answers will vary. Grace and peace are experienced together.

9. a. "I give you peace. Don't worry or fear."

b. "Be at peace." Jesus has made the things of this world irrelevant.

c. The prophets have misled people by claiming peace when there is no peace—by whitewashing a wall to make it look good when in fact it will soon fall.

10. a. The picture is of pairs that obviously are never found in the world as we know it: a wolf and a lamb, a leopard with a goat, a lion

and a calf, all being led by a child. This is the peace of "one day," when the earth is full of the knowledge of the Lord.

b. Answers will vary. Can this kind of peace be yours today in the problems you face if you rely on the wisdom of the Lord?

Session 7: Stocking Up on the Fruit of the Spirit, Part 2

1. a. God may be showing patience to the objects of His wrath (sinners) in order to make His glory and grace known to us.

b. Jesus has unlimited patience for me so that others will believe in Him and come to know Him and have eternal life.

c. God is being patient so that people won't perish. He's giving people a chance to repent. His patience will mean salvation for some.

2. a. and b. Answers will vary.

c. ". . . with all humility and gentleness, with patience, bearing with one another in love . . ." (Ephesians 4:2)

3. a. Answers will vary.

b. No one is righteous, no one is good. No one is kind on her own. All have turned away from God.

c. God's kindness does not appear because of what we have done, but because of His mercy.

d. We can clothe ourselves in kindness by bearing with one another and forgiving as God has forgiven us.

4. a. A good tree will bear good fruit; a bad tree cannot.

b. He encourages people; he is filled with the Holy Spirit and with faith. The fruit is that a number of people are brought to the Lord.

c. God equips us with everything good to do His will through Christ Jesus.

d. Answers will vary.

5. a. "Be faithful unto death, and I will give you the crown of life."

b. It's believing in things we can't see.

c. It comes to us by the grace of God.

d. It comes to us from Jesus.

6. a. We suffer grief in trials so that our faith may be proved genuine and may result in praise and glory and honor when Jesus is revealed.

b. Since God is already all knowing, we don't need to prove anything to Him. Perhaps God is proving to us that our faith is genuine. It's one thing to say I have a deep, abiding faith; it's another to know it for sure because I have gone through a trial that I could only have survived because of God's faithfulness to me.

c. "Extinguish all the flaming darts of the evil one." Satan wants nothing more than for me to doubt God, and he'll do what he can to try and make this happen.

7. a. The Lord leads the humble and teaches them His way.

b. "The meek shall inherit the land," and as they do, they'll enjoy peace.

c. Serving Christ is, in itself, a source of comfort to us.

8. a. All that striving is tiring. Keeping up appearances will wear you out!

b. and c. Answers will vary.

d. God opposes the proud, but He gives grace to the humble. Perhaps this is the origin of the saying "Pride goeth before a fall." You can either humble yourself, or God will humble you. (See Isaiah 42:8.) God will lift you up in due time. You can cast all your anxiety on Him "because He cares for you" (v. 7).

9. a. Answers will vary.

b. God has the power to bring everything under His control. He can transform my lowly body, whereas by myself, I am unable to transform anything.

10. We will "walk by the Spirit." In other words, we will strive to lead a God-pleasing life.

Session 8: Take Me Away

1. a. The Spirit of God

b. God's breath, as He breathes life into us

2. Answers will vary.

3. a. Elijah had just slaughtered all the prophets of Baal (1 Kings 18:40), and Jezebel vows to do the same to him.

b. Elijah is afraid and runs for his life.

c. Lot is told by the angels to flee for his life, as Sodom and Gomorrah are about to be destroyed.

d. Answers will vary.

4. a. Essentially, Elijah says, "I've had enough, Lord."

b. "Why are you doing this Lord? Didn't I do everything You asked me to? I've had enough, Lord! If You are going to treat me like this, just kill me!"

c. Answers will vary. Though I've not asked for God to just go ahead and kill me now, I've definitely "cried uncle" and told God I've had enough.

5. a. It's not healthy to push ourselves too hard. God wants His children to sleep.

b. Answers will vary.

6. Food and water

7. a. He found a cave and stayed there.

b. Moses, tending his sheep there, had a visit from God in a burning bush.

c. Mount Horeb and Mount Sinai are the same mountain. It is on this mountain that Moses asks to see God's glory. While God says that no one can look on Him and live, yet He will place Moses in the cleft of the rock and cover him until He has passed by.

8. a. "What are you doing here, Elijah?"

b. When God asks, "What are you doing here, Elijah?" Elijah responds with a litany of despair. He feels alone, rejected, abandoned by God.

c. While Elijah doesn't ask to see God's glory (and from his attitude, I'm not sure he feels there's anything glorious about God right now), God tells him to go stand on the mountain before the Lord.

9. a. A great wind tears up the mountain, breaking the rocks.

b. and c. Answers will vary.

d. Elijah pulls his cloak over his face and goes to stand before God. It's apparent that Elijah remembered God's word to Moses that no one can look on God and live. It's also apparent that he knows God has shown up, and in a big way, despite the quiet voice.

e. Moses, too, hid his face when God appeared in the burning bush.

f. God listens again to Elijah's complaints. This time He tells Elijah to go back home, to anoint a new ruler, to anoint a new prophet (so he knows he's not in it alone, and so there is someone to take over his ministry)—and oh, by the way, there are still seven thousand in Israel who have *not* bowed to Baal. God gives him step-by-step directions. He promises to provide for Elijah, and He does!

10. a. "A sound like a mighty, rushing wind"

b. They were filled with the Holy Spirit and began speaking in tongues.

c. Three thousand people were added to the Kingdom. They devoted themselves to meeting together, eating together, praying together, and hearing God's Word in the form of teaching from those who knew Him best. They gave to those who had need, and they praised God.

d. Answers will vary.